KANT

PICTURES OF CZECH POSTMODERISM

JIŘÍ PŘIBÁŇ

PICTURES OF CZECH POSTMODERNISM

JIŘÍ PŘIBÁŇ

Contents:

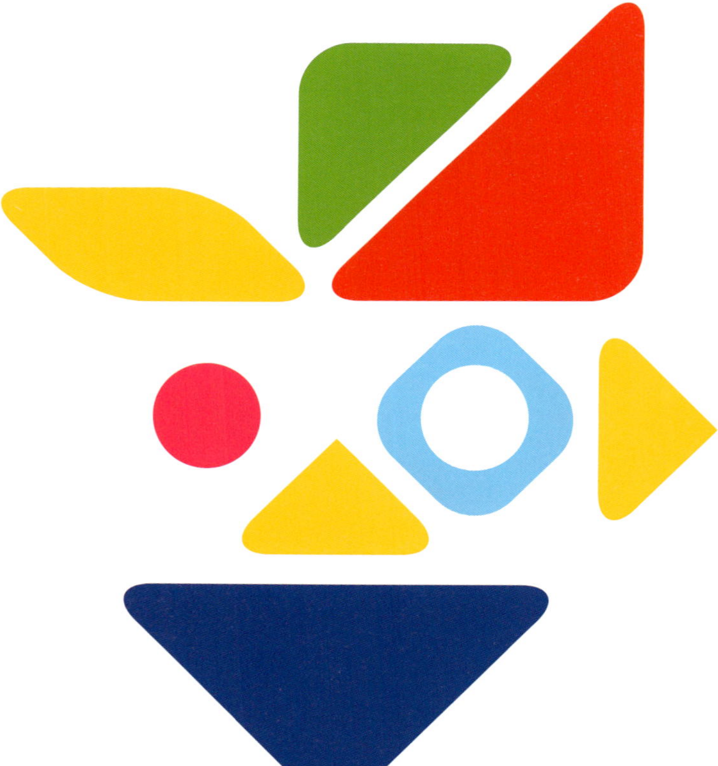

Jiří Přibáň
Preface to the English edition

What can be read from a book about Czech postmodern art that is no specialized text, consisting instead of essays on individual artists and the author's personal reflections? In the contemporary global art flow, overloaded with freely available digital information from any culture and subculture in every corner of our planet, is there anything left to communicate? Perhaps the seemingly marginal deliberations on art that have arisen and continue to arise in one of the Central European cultures where the distinction between cultural centres and their peripheries is so intensely felt yet, paradoxically, also blurred?

The essays in this book deal with those who currently figure among the most important Czech artists and whose work is internationally recognized. Most of them entered the art scene in the late 1980s on the crest of a powerful generational wave known as Czech postmodernism. Although this artistic drive ran parallel to revolutionary changes in Central and Eastern Europe, it would be grossly simplistic and misleading to view Czech postmodernism as a by-product of the disintegration of Communist regimes and exposure to the effects of West European culture. In fact, the story of Czech postmodernism is unique evidence that, in diverse social and political contexts, artists ultimately address issues of a general nature beyond politics and ideology.

This book primarily discusses how art, as an original form of aesthetic thinking, has been manifested in the specific context of Czech society over the past two decades. Jiří David's "semantic soups", in which individual symbols lose their established meanings, and Tomáš Císařovský's "red deserts", in which apparent civilized and technological refinement uncovers profound violence, theft and cultural ambivalence, are both generally comprehensible and clearer than at the time of their creation. Universally communicable are the postmodern variations on the ideal image in the work of Antonín Střížek, Jan Merta's exploration of the transcending conditions of imagery, the post-Renaissance ingenuity of Petr Nikl, the combination of avant-garde language and shameless decoration in the visual manifestations of Petr Písařík, Stanislav Diviš's systemic puzzles in abstract painting, and the uncompromising pop-culture and pop-politics comments in the paintings and actions of Ostrava's Jiří Surůvka.

Unlike the generation of Young British Artists (YBA), the representatives of Czech postmodernism lacked the machinery of media advertising, scandal and artificially produced generational unity. What was scandalous about Czech artists was that, towards the end of totalitarian society, they dared to work quite freely, regardless of binding political ideology or cultural, artistic or commercial programmes. Czech postmodern artistic expression has thus always been free of the dictate of the moment and the related media provocation that is so typical of today's digitized society and its liquid culture. For Czech artists, artistic narcissism did not become a method of self-propaganda, as is common in today's impersonal yet more authenticity-obsessed world, but remained the subject of self-irony.

It is therefore no coincidence that the art works of Czech postmodernism often give a more focused, concentrated impression compared to foreign works. However, Czech artists are associated with the postmodern turn in art and Western culture because of distrust of "grand narratives" and avant-garde gestures, and because of the ability to convincingly challenge certain key aesthetic distinctions, such as high and low culture, art and kitsch or pure forms and decoration. Due to this combination of peculiar visual expression and general aesthetic and intellectual background, Czech postmodernism became a timeless phenomenon deserving attention in the context of contemporary European and world art.

Finally, I want to thank Barbora Donathová, Daniel Donath, Karel Kerlický, Martin Kroupa, Alexandr Mareš, Magda Nováková, Radek Pokorný, Lenka Suchánková, the Pierstone law firm, Petr Písařík and the other artists discussed in these essays for their generous support and extraordinary help and assistance leading to the successful publication of this book.

Cardiff, 10 August 2013

Jiří Přibáň

A Few Personal Words by Way of Introduction

The notes and observations for these essays were made slowly and by degrees over a period stretching back to 2003; the vast majority of the texts were then published in final form between 2008 and 2010. Initially, there was no organized or pre-arranged method to my writing, which was essentially my own particular way of coping with my new life abroad. The joy of having this opportunity to discover a new culture and way of life and thinking in the British Isles was never able to suppress completely how I felt about losing daily contact with cultural events at home.

This drove me to consider all the more intensely what I would single out as unique and important in contemporary Czech culture from both a general and a personal perspective. I found myself gravitating towards Czech postmodernism because, in part, this art played a key role for me during my university studies and, therefore, as I was maturing intellectually and culturally. Much like alternative music concerts, unofficial art exhibitions were an opportunity for us to look around ourselves unfettered and to find meaningfulness in the middle of all-pervasive cynicism and the spreading cultural junk of late socialist society. Visiting these exhibitions, concerts and theatrical performances was an expression of a special instinct of cultural self-preservation.

After 1989, it was interesting to see how this alternative culture gradually established itself, passing general post-Communist taste and culture on the way. Everyone expected change, but there was none; instead, the cultural conservatism strongly rooted in Czech society prevailed. Although the generation of Czech postmodernism has had a major influence on the art scene in the past twenty years, it has not become a widely accepted cultural canon or norm.

Writing essays on individual artists, while not exactly therapeutic, was certainly an archaeological dig into my own cultural and intellectual history. Against this personal backdrop, I tried to capture cultural constants and variables in Czech society over the last twenty years. By no means is this an exercise in art history or a sketch of sociology and critical theory of contemporary art. The reader should not be surprised that certain names are missing or that younger artists not emerging on the Czech art scene until the 1990s stand shoulder to shoulder with the leading lights of the Tvrdohlaví [The Hardheads] group. This is no expert study organizing, cataloguing and categorically arranging historical and current events in the Czech art scene. It is not my intention to write "neutrally", and my observations are certainly not made with aloofness, detachment, or any other neutralizing "distance". Rather, I am quite biased, not only because the works I have covered in this book were crucial in shaping my personal beliefs and overall view of art. I have a personal and friendly relationship with each of the artists whose work is discussed in this book; often, the bond is so strong that I am highly vexed if I miss them on one of my visits to Prague, which are so fleeting these days, but I then look forward to the next trip all the more eagerly. I appreciate these personal ties enormously and, of course, I am grateful that my friends have gradually allowed me to glimpse their creative worlds, ideas and processes.

Nevertheless, I would argue that these essays are not some personal declaration of admiration for a particular artist, but an attempt at examining in detail the general motives and reasons for underpinning why I consider a specific artefact important and significant. In my writing, I always start with the general and make my way towards the specific. I am keen to capture how, in the visual arts as a sovereign form of symbolic expression, philosophical thoughts or spiritual experiences, political views and the cultural and historical memory are manifested, along with purely specific phenomena such as the playfulness or unrestrained imagination of inventors and hobbyists.

In each of the essays, I focus on a particular context of contemporary art, while trying to steer clear of any reductive interpretation of a particular work. In the essay on Tomáš Císařovský, I concentrate primarily on the collective memory and the ability of art to serve up to society, and to question, images of its own history. In the case of Stanislav Diviš, on the other hand, any such reconstruction of the past is subordinate from the outset to the strict logic of the aesthetic system.

Provocative context and the ability to break up deftly any system of social and aesthetic conventions and characteristics are exceptional, in a Czech context, to Jiří David, and therefore I used this strategy as a basis in my essay devoted to his work. Human playfulness, childish imagination and inventiveness were the starting point of my essay on the work of Petr Nikl, but that is by no means to say that it eschews a a transcending eye and inner voice, which, conversely, were emphasized in the text devoted to the paintings of Jan Merta. The ability to recycle materials and combine high avant-garde art with seemingly debased decorativeness, which I chose as a basis in my discussion on the work of Petr Písařík, could certainly also be attributed to other artists covered by this book. Jiří Surůvka is not only an amazing performer, but also has the extraordinary ability to confront pop-art and pop-politics in their darkest, demonic context. Finally, for the work of Antonín Střížek, I opted for an openly philosophical context, although we are sure to find similarities, for example, between his work and that of Tomáš Císařovský, which could bring the whole story of "post-modern Czech paintings" full circle, returning us to the point where we started.

Although I refer to art, by turns, as "collective memory", a "system", "anaesthetics", "playfulness", "recycling", "transcendence", "unrest" and "philosophy", I have consciously sought to avoid any dogmatism. Rather, I use these contexts as variations on the theme of artistic expression as a particular kind of thinking. This theme also appears in the final interview for the periodical Umělec [Artist], in which, thanks to the extremely intelligent and appreciative approach of the editor, Ivan Mečl, topical and timeless questions on the problems of artistic creation and the status of the artist in society are featured side by side. I greatly respect his friendship and admire everything that this humble man, one of the few genuine bohemians, has achieved for art in the Czech Republic and elsewhere in the world over the past 20 years.

I also appreciate the young artist Karel Štědrý for the care, discretion and commitment with which he has undertaken the hard work on the artistic design of this book. In my opinion, he found an original solution to the problem of how to connect eight bold, distinctive and in many respects different figures on the contemporary Czech art scene by employing the system and aesthetics of an ancient puzzle, the tangram, which originated more than a thousand years ago in China. He had to add an eighth tan (geometric shape) to the square, traditionally divided into seven parts, to make it match the number of essays in the book. This systemic stylization, verging on naive street art and conceptual art, imparts lightness and playfulness without clouding the seriousness of the individual topics or conflicting with the aesthetic code of the artists to whom this book is dedicated. I think the visual appearance of the book is itself a distinctive image of the new-generation Czech postmodernism. The publication of this book would not have been possible without certain friends and people who, even in these economically uncertain times, generously donated production funds. I would like to thank, in particular, Radek Pokorný from the law firm Pokorný, Wagner a spol., and Alexandr Mareš from Mareš Partners, who, when the situation was at its bleakest, offered financial assistance without any hesitation. I am equally grateful to Martin Kroupa from JBC and Lenka Suchánková from the Pierstone law firm, who also donated considerable funds towards this costly book, and I am grateful to the Prinz Prager Gallery for the same support. I would also like to thank Karel Kerlický, with whom everything was organized via cross-Channel phone calls, whose publishing experience has been indispensable for everything of worth in this book. I thank the editing team of the Salon supplement to the Právo daily newspaper, where most of the essays were originally published, and in particular Alice Šimonová for her critical advice, editorial work and the care she devoted to all the texts.

Cardiff, 25 October 2010

PICTURES OF CZECH POSTMODERNISM
THE ANOMIC SOCIETY OF LATE SOCIALISM

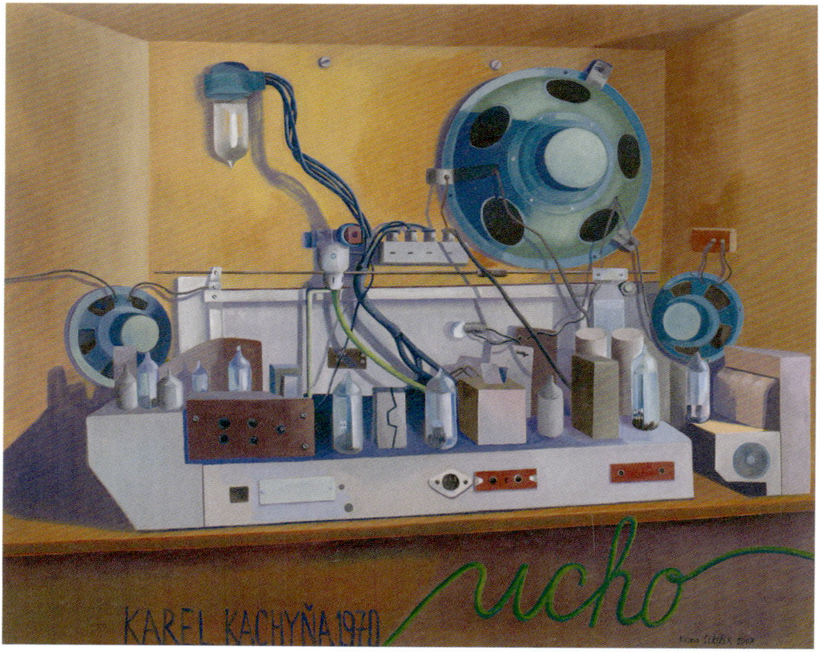
KAREL KACHYŇA 1970
ucho

Pictures of Czech Postmodernism

The anomic society of late socialism

In the 1980s, Czech society was dominated by general *anomie*. This situation, where official norms and cultural values cease to apply and tension keeps intensifying between personal talent and the opportunity to find an outlet for it in society, naturally had features specific to the period. In the Normalization era of the 1970s and 1980s, the ruling Communist elite no longer had an ideological vision, just a state welfare plan and a socialist version of consumer society intended to drum up public loyalty to the regime. This peculiar form of governance was based on the idea that politics can be the preserve of a narrow party elite, while the bare bones of welfare would keep the people in their allotments and weekend cottages and stop them from demonstrating in the squares and protesting in the streets.

Yet an integral part of this consumer "paradise it is to see" was the humiliating queues under real socialism, in which people had to wait their turn to obtain, with a bit of luck, "dream" – preferably "Western" – products. This transformation of the people into a shapeless, mob-minded and -acting mass, was captured with precision, for example, by the Russian writer Vladimir Sorokin in the mid-1980s in his experimental novel *The Queue*, in which none of the indeterminate, socially faded characters knows what they are actually waiting for and whether they will need it, but, just like everyone else, they want it anyway. Standing in a queue is a special form of socialist pornography blurring the distinction between the academic and the animal. Although the police ostensibly organize the queue, it is obvious that the most effective means of control is to leave the queue to itself. People voluntarily and gladly stand in a queue, and thus are in a position where they scrutinize and keep an eye on each other.

This situation may have made it easier for the ruling powers to keep the population under general surveillance, but it also provoked a more pronounced counter-movement in which people nurtured their

Antonín Střížek, Ear, 2007

talents independently of the official culture and politics. Those who chose to ignore the ever larger and more frequent queues of decaying state socialism preferred the opportunity for creative personal and self-expression rather than the passivity of hanging around in queues waiting for anything, anywhere, any time. As the American sociologist Robert Merton would say, in the anomic Czech society of the 1980s, the rebels slowly began to vanquish the conformists, forging new cultural and artistic codes as they did so.

Revolt of the stomach, artistic rebels

This movement was most noticeable, naturally, in the arts, where the first and highest prize is the very chance to demonstrate one's own talents and create a work that is simultaneously personal, original and able to make an impression on others. Artistic codes were not superficially political; their sights were trained much more on society itself, of which these rebellious artists had become increasingly ashamed. The political system failed to reproduce itself and, if anything, was a mockery, whereas the social reality had become increasingly loathsome. The Polish poet Czesław Miłosz once called this strange state of resistance to totalitarianism the "revolt of the stomach".

In the 1980s, when fear of police repression was gradually fading, the lower organs of the digestive and urinary tract could remain quite calm, but the stomach revolted all the more. Art was swayed not by political ethos, but much more by feelings of general shame, anger or even disgust. For example, the performances by the Cellar Theatre (*Divadlo Sklep*) and Tomáš Vorel's film debut "Prague Five" were typified by grimacing and the almost lascivious exploration of the official socialist pop culture and its ideological basis. Sometimes it was funny, other times unbearably embarrassing and unprofessional, but always worth seeing. The shows were even therapeutic in one sense because, here, we did not discover only that famous "inner imbecile", so popular among theatre-goers, but could see imbeciles everywhere around us.

An end to the Czech Grotesque

Unlike the theatre, artists starting out at this time had to deal with other artistic problems and devise different visual codes because grimaces and parody were the truest expressions of the "Czech Grotesque" from the 1970s, as captured in their best paintings, installations and sculptures by Jiří Načeradský, Jiří Sopko, Karel Nepraš, Kurt Gebauer and other "Grotesque" artists. While the art generation emerging in the 1980s was able to ignore official art completely, it had to be all the more critical in dealing with this very strong tradition of unofficial, and for that reason more respected, art and its existential expression, the ability to capture the absurdity of the world and socially critical poignancy. At that time, it was entirely unnecessary to waste energy on confronting the official nonsense. It was more important to review and challenge what was then considered meaningful and alternative art.

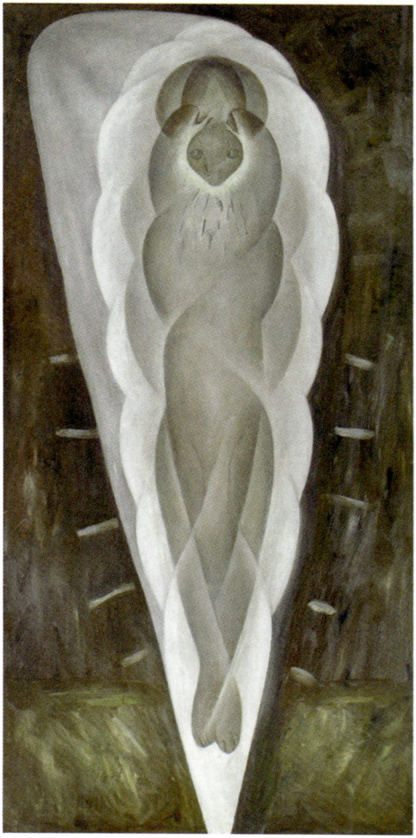

Petr Nikl, *Birth of the Cat*, 1987

From the end of the 1960s, the Czech Grotesque had continued Central European cultural traditions, and therefore audiences had the impression that it was very natural and deeply rooted in the Czech environment, that it belonged to the European cultural canon, and that it was the right alternative to the official artistic and political baggage of the time. It may have required even more courage to make a stand against this strong artistic and cultural tradition than to ostentatiously ignore the official artistic flow of late-Normalization society. Nevertheless, it was possible because ironic expression at that time already often served only as an excuse and justification of individual and collective failures and weaknesses.

The fine dividing line between irony and cynicism was upset in the 1980s as Czech society became generally rougher and number. The Czech Grotesque thus ultimately became, against its will, a hostage to those who needed the assurance that their personal failures are just one of many manifestations of the general absurdity of the world, about which no one can do anything. When absurdity is normal, it is possible to get accustomed to absurd Normalization while mocking it without feeling that we are laughing, above all, at ourselves and our own abominations. The original barbs of the Grotesque lost their sharpness over time, and therefore it was necessary to look for other artistic codes.

Another area against which young artists had to rail in the 1980s was not connected at all with the domestic environment, but concerned global trends. As elsewhere in the world, in the Czech environment the new generation rejected minimalism, dominant until then, whose concept of aesthetic reduction had been completely exhausted. Indeed, at that time even the American composer Philip Glass had revised his systematically minimalist music entirely and radically affiliated it with the tradition of Late Romanticism. Similar romanticizing shifts can also be found in the musical compositions of Gavin Bryars and in the art works of Frank Stella, who, in the 1980s, embarked on a path of open decorativeness and began calling for the revival of Baroque traditions in plastic art.

Imagery and emotional charge ceased to be crimes. Quite the reverse, as they became part and parcel of artistic expression. The emerging generation of Czech artists was therefore able to find its own voice and expression in the European and global context, which, during the era of the politically divided world, heralded the synergies and spatial illimitability of today's global artistic canon.

Confrontations and the paths of Czech postmodernism

The six *Confrontations* group exhibitions, whose main organizers in the mid-1980s were Jiří David and Stanislav Diviš, were instrumental in forming the aesthetic backdrop, ideas and expression (or perhaps expressions) of this generation of artists and were much more important than, for example, the subsequent establishment of the small *Tvrdohlaví* group. In one interview, Stanislav Diviš described this complex cultural movement as a bunch of guys who discovered that, in some vile Communist housing estate, someone had made a pitch which, during the Communist timelessness, had been left untended until it became a heap of rubble. These boys decided that they would use this space and restore it so that they would be able to start playing the games they themselves enjoyed. Sometimes the foul-mouthed security guard would run along and confiscate their ball or tell them to go somewhere else, but someone always ran home for a new ball so that they could start playing again.

I have no idea if Stanislav Diviš was aware of Kurt Vonnegut's division of people into those who want to play games and those who believe their life mission is to spoil those games, but that is exactly what the situation was like in Czech art and throughout society. This was perhaps one of the factors behind the formation, in the late 1980s, of a very strong and highly diverse artistic wave which encompassed not only the members of *Tvrdohlaví* or artists emerging later on in the 1990s who were associated with Galerie MXM, such as Tomáš Císařovský, Jiří Kovan-

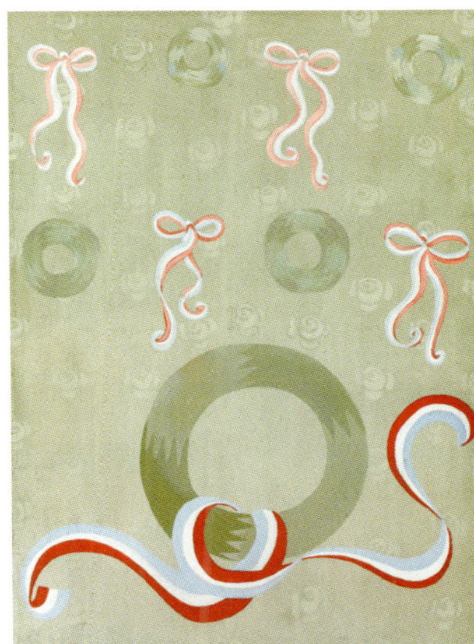

Jiří David, On Roses, 1989

da, Jan Merta and Antonín Střížek, but also the likes of Jiří Surůvka, Petr Lysáček, Petr Písařík and others who were not even 30 years old in 1989. Since 1990, when some of the above artists participated in the groundbreaking collective exhibition *Paths of Postmodernism*, this artistic and generational wave started to be dubbed "Czech postmodernism". Even this short list of names shows that this extremely vital generation is of absolutely crucial importance for both the recent history and the present-day situation of Czech art.

History, its symbols and narratives

Despite its considerable diversity, Czech postmodernism has always been characterized primarily by the revival of historicity and transcen-

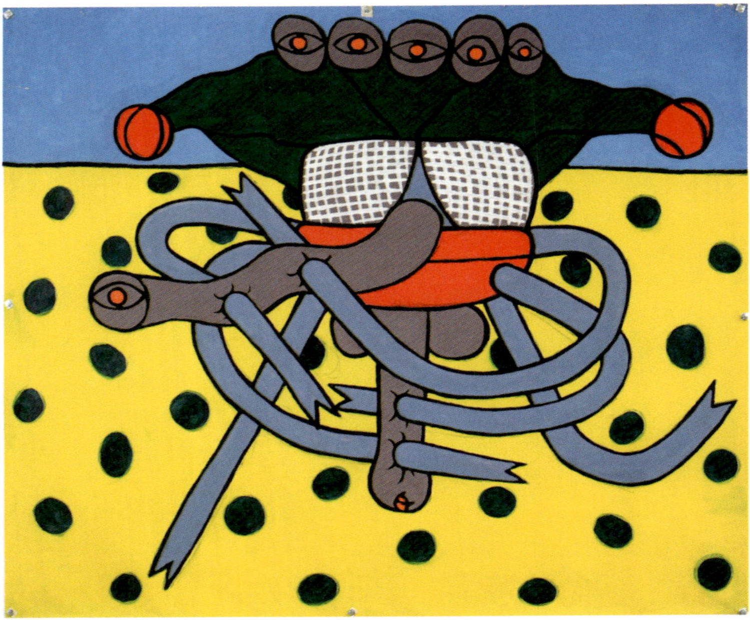

Casper the Soloist 85 (Bystroš), 1985

dence in artistic expression. The return to symbolic imagery and to the epic concept of painting, including prehistoric and archetypal themes, is closely related to this. Suffering is no longer associated with imagery, having been replaced by unrestricted imagination and refined semantic games.

In a society constantly overloaded with vacant political symbols and officially approved national myths, series of works by Jiří David unexpectedly appeared in which the theme of home and national history, as well as folk decorations, is treated originally, without any link to the "permitted" meanings. It was as though all those familiar symbols and concepts were suddenly floating in a state of political weightlessness.

In his early works, Stanislav Diviš, with similar levity, but by no means superficially, incorporated the themes of archetypal images of the landscape, "heavenly gates", the ships of the Argonauts and other mythological references. He used this historicizing perspective as the basis for radical artistic stylization. Diviš subsequently perfected this method of converting a historical theme into a general system of visual signs, for example, in the *Remnants* series, in which fabric samplers from an abandoned textile factory in the borderlands became the basis for his sovereign abstract painting.

History as a subject and the problem of reconstructing the past has always been a central motif even for the much more epic artistic expression of Tomáš Císařovský. In his series *From the Diary of My Grandfather the Legionnaire*, he emphasizes the travel motif and conceives history as both a historical narrative and a moral challenge that needs to be thought and talked about constantly, including by artistic means.

Czech postmodernism was thus able to capture, alongside monumental history, such as the maps and boundaries of the Czechoslovak Republic, the history of everyday life in its banal yet admirable simplicity. And all these pictures were supremely subversive because they were created and had an effect completely independent of the officially canonized ideological interpretation of history. Whereas David was interested primarily in the social explosiveness of historical symbols and Diviš examined them as a possible basis for the creative stylization and design of a visual system, Císařovský has always remained on a plane where stories of the past become history – on the plane of historical narratives.

The meaning of history and transcendence

The question of the meaning of history inherently includes the possibility of transcendence, evident, for example, in the sophisticatedly retrospective painting of Antonín Střížek. First Republic photography here comes back to life in newly conceived oil paintings in which objectivity, entirely in the spirit of postmodernism, becomes distinctive decoration.

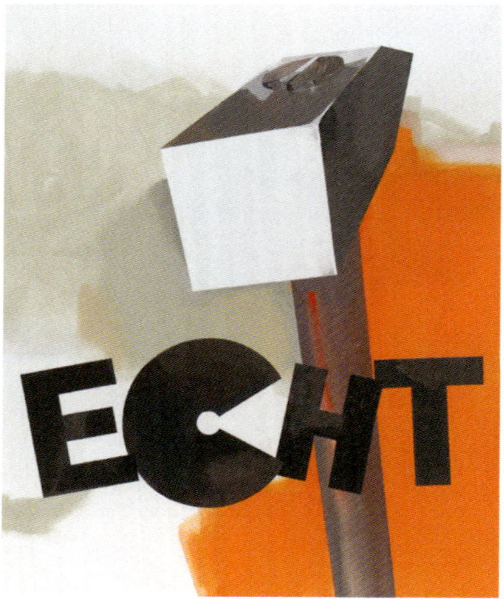

Reflections on the past form the basis for semantic play in the artistic present. Every mythology is immediately and deliberately falsified artistic fantasy, as in Borges's stories. While we never fully understand archetypes and mythologies, this gives us all the more opportunity to reduce their semantic charge again and again and use them for our own artistic designs.

Artwork is then simultaneously a disciplined performance and an adventure, in which we do not know exactly how and in what way the final shape and form will speak to the audience. As shown, for example, by the philosophically reduced and refined canvases of Jan Merta, we are faced by recognition of the boundaries of our knowledge and, at the same time, by the ability to push back those boundaries and deal with their lines, whether visual or conceptual.

It is here that we also need to seek out the transition, where the historicizing and archetypally pseudo-historicizing views we saw in

Jan Merta, Echt II, 2008

the images Jaroslav Róna and other members of *Tvrdohlaví* in the late 1980s made the jump to a game of pure imagination and fantasy. In this regard, for example, Petr Nikl's early canvases continue to stand out, in which biomorphic depictions of the themes of birth, hatching and growth in themselves contain both the mythological circularity of archetypal images and the immediacy of children's toys. Born or unborn cats, lions, moths and other creatures are indeed of this world, but the process of hatching and birth is something that transcends this world and that can be captured only by way of an image that has a similar capacity for transcendence.

A work is specific, the message general: external influences and originality in Czech postmodernism

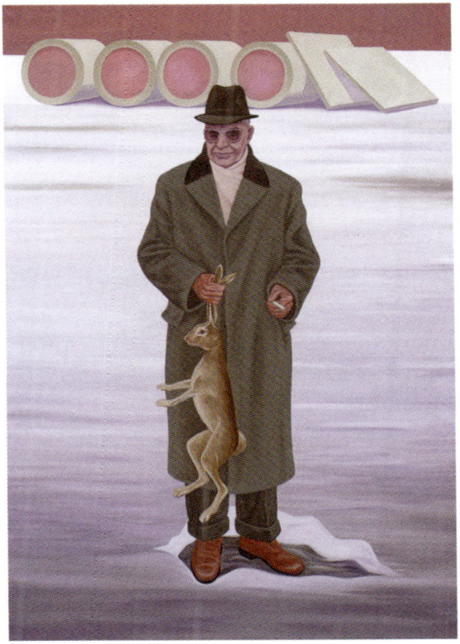

Semantic games with historical themes and symbols, the rehabilitation of archetypal expressions, wild imagination and the shameless interlinking of banality and spiritual kitsch with various forms of knowledge and understanding, all this connected Czech postmodernism from the beginning with European and world art. As a result, the local art scene always reflected the influence of the Italian transvantgarde, the German *Junge Wilde* and US realism inspired by pop-art, but this was never epigonism or the mere following of general trends. Nor was there ever any empty play with kitsch, which is often how postmodernism was characterized in Western Europe and in the United States. It was as if the local artists were well aware that such play would only lead to the

Tomaš Císařovský, Hunting, 2008

boundless creation of further kitsch and that art, while it should not be embarrassingly didactic or moralizing, should also never be completely frivolous and reduced to a joke or a momentary idea, no matter how original.

Every artistic movement and the general development of art includes the coded tendency to copy patterns and follow the major trends. Whether the path followed is that beaten by the French Impressionists, the Spanish surrealist school or American abstract expressionism, even in art the world seems to be divided into those who lead and those who follow. Yet the fundamental imperative of modern art is for every artist's output to be, in particular, original, unmistakable and inseparably connected with his or her person. Avoiding epigonism and finding original expression in a sea of general developmental trends is often a very painful and not always a successful process, as shown by the stories of many artists, one Czech historical example being Emil Filla.

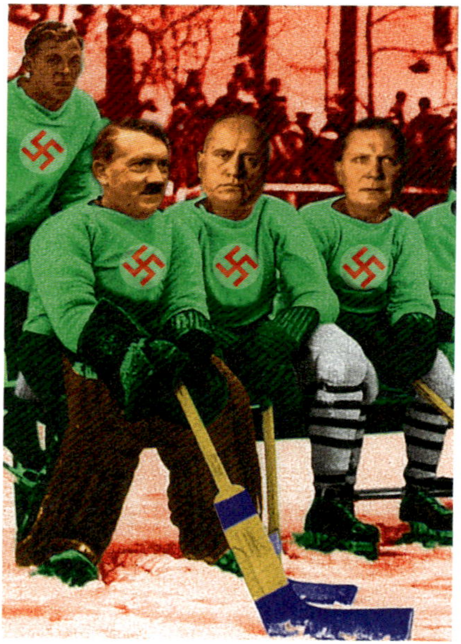

On the whole, Czech postmodernism managed to avoid the trap of epigonism by embarking on its own path in exploring themes and solutions to problems that were of key importance in relation to the specific place and time in which these artists were operating. It was as if they were reaffirming that aesthetic judgements and thoughts are always specific and not subject to any general verdicts, criteria or conceptual trends.

Although the work is always specific, the message must be general. If a work of art is to transcend the time and place of its creation, the

Jiří Surůvka, The German Men's Hockey Team 1936, 1998

inner tension of artistic output must be handled successfully, as is evident from the life's work of Georgia O'Keeffe, who, in the 1920s, emerged from the cultural periphery of Wisconsin to teach European snobs about the art of abstraction, paving the way for the development of fine arts in the United States for decades to come.

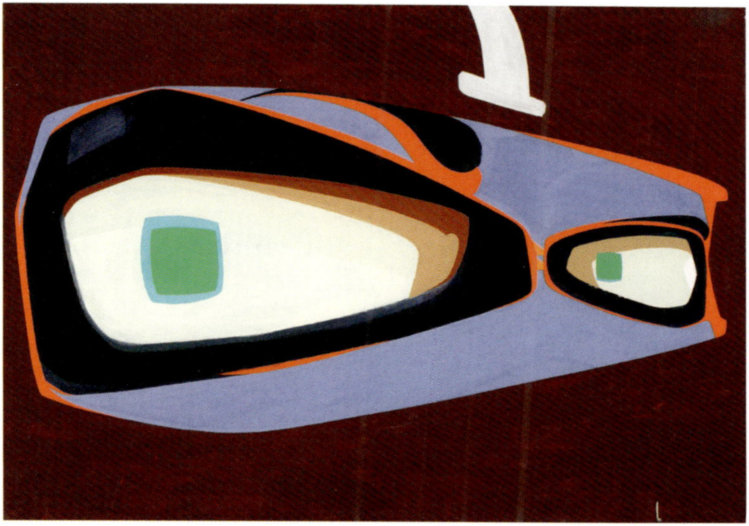

The critical function of imagery

Similarly, the best Czech postmodernists managed to capture the general atmosphere of the time but go their own way and describe what was unique in the place and time in which they lived and worked. In this sense, they avoided postmodern posturing with gestures declaring the "death of the author" or "death of the subject", as was once a fashionable trend, especially in literature and conceptual art. If anything, traces of postmodernism in the Czech environment left the

Petr Písařík, Schumacher, 2001

question of "Who is the author?" and what is his or her role in a given situation. This was no quest in search of the authenticity of artistic expression, but the artist's attempt at a description, in reverse, of his/her own creation, which is also a special "description of a struggle". Yet what sort of struggle was it and against whom did it, and does it still, have to be waged? What was the critical dimension of Czech postmodernism?

The life of anomic Czech society in the late 1980s was affected not only by empty political-party rituals, but also by an impersonal government of incompetent bureaucracy which no longer understood its own language and own commands. Not only the government, but the whole of society, gradually lost its general capacity for mutual communication and imagination, without which, of course, art, and life itself, is impossible. Opposing such a social morass with the power of postmodern imagery was then a supreme manifestation of social and political criticism. The socially critical function of art does not lie in the reproduction of ideological tracts and political dictates, but in the much more authentic joy from the freedom of artistic creation, which is inherently unpredictable, unsecured, and therefore so adventurous and revelatory.

Even though Czech postmodernism is now primarily a historical theme, the force with which it managed to formulate a basic background and aesthetic principles of visual arts in the second half of the 1980s and, subsequently, in the 1990s in the conditions of a free democratic society, radically changed Czech society's artistic and political codes. And if we trace contemporary art and its own means of expression and communication codes, we see how they still resonate with the aesthetic basis formulated by the Czech postmodernist generation twenty years ago.

HISTORY AND LANDSCAPES OF "HUMAN RESOURCES"

HISTORICAL MEANING AND UNDERSTANDING OF THE PRESENT IN THE WORK OF TOMÁŠ CÍSAŘOVSKÝ

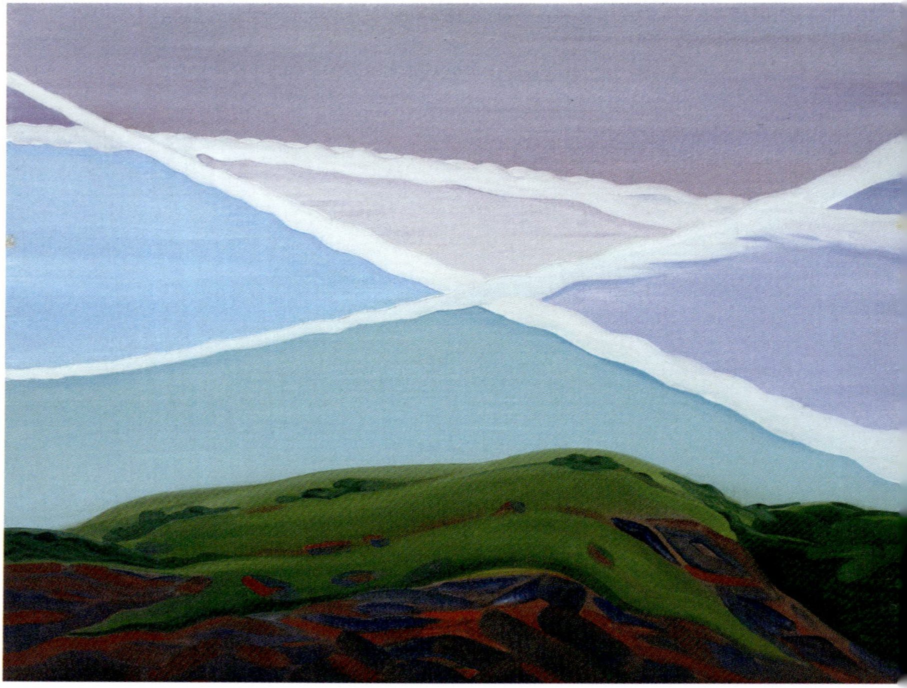

History and Landscapes of "Human Resources"

Historical Meaning and Understanding of the Present in the Work of Tomáš Císařovský

Divoká Šárka (*Wild Šárka*), by the painter Tomáš Císařovský, is disturbing not in its form, but in the intensity of content. In the lower third of the canvas, the iconic shape of the hill – well known to everyone in Prague seeking respite among the last scraps of nature in the capital – is captured in an array of grey, brown and green. Císařovský's bold line and rich colours admirably portray the pre-civilization monumentality of the nature here while combining the half-forgotten history of this Prague hill with the noisiest, proudest manifestation of our technical civilization. Namely, the upper two thirds of the canvas are dominated by slightly undulating vapour trails left in the sky by an overhead aircraft – the symbol of how we have overcome even that most fundamental of natural human limitations, the law of gravity. From above, then, emissions and waste from manmade creations relentlessly rain down on the *remnants of nature* at Divoká Šárka. Whereas the cold grey canyon provided protection to our forebears over a thousand years ago, these days aircraft pass over the same spot as they take off and land, and it is becoming increasingly obvious that not even humankind can save nature from them and other technical inventions.

The view of those three intersecting lines, splitting the skies above Císařovský's Divoká Šárka into larger and smaller sections, is reminiscent of Heidegger's account of modern technology exhorting nature to supply energy. There is a significant difference between a jet plane, the operation of which depends on the discovery of oil and its extraction from underground deposits, and a windmill, whose sails, though rotating in the wind, do not consume energy from the airflow; rather, when they are done with it, they pass it on downwind. What sets current technology apart from all humankind's previous instruments and inventions is the fact that it accumulates, restructures, distributes

Tomáš Císařovský, Divoká Šárka (Wild Šárka), 2005

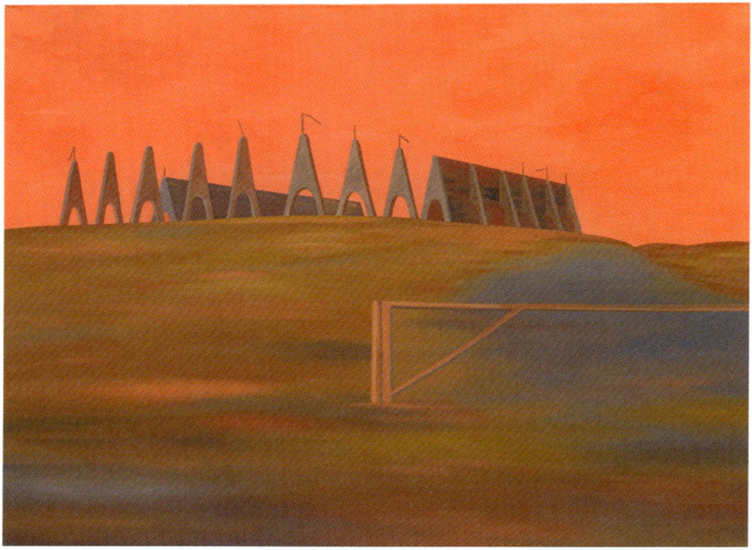

and transforms natural energy. It utilizes and processes everything to do with nature, man himself and his ever faster, electronified and digitally convertible culture. The colour (this is perhaps Císařovský's most important means of expression) of the sky he also depicts changes in each of the fields demarcated by the jet engine fumes, passing from turquoise into azure and on into a menacing purple. In postmodern saturated times not even the sky has its own colour!

The picture described is part of *Holidays in Bohemia*, a series created between 2004 and 2006 that is dedicated to the Czech landscape and its modern transformation by civilization. On another canvas, then, the same vapour trails eloquently descend on Točník Castle. The motif of another picture is a gas tank in the vicinity of a plastic swimming pool, that symbol of Czech wealth in the 1990s. Instead of the civilist poetry we know, for example, from the paintings of Kamil Lhoták, Jan Smetana, František Gross and other members of Group 42 (*Skupina 42*),

Tomáš Císařovský, Líbeznice, 2004

fear and uncertainty prevail here. What sort of era is this, where humans can cut through the sky in machines? What sort of energy are we actually keeping in reservoirs and storage facilities, the destination of the gas and heat pipelines devastating the alluvial landscape of Central Bohemia, and what is the point of exploiting the natural resources we transmit in this manner? And where are those whose civilization can change the face of ostensibly eternal nature so rapidly and so radically? Why does the painter wilfully ignore them throughout the series?

One answer is offered by the eloquent *Líbeznice*, where concrete columns and an empty silage pit rise against a reddish sky, while a gate looms in a deserted field in the foreground. This is the Stonehenge of Czech capitalism at the beginning of the third millennium! Or is it the equivalent of the space monolith in Clarke's (and Kubrick's) *2001: A Space Odyssey*? Are not those poles also some kind of starting point of civilization, like Clarke's monolith, which absorbs light and also emits its own active energy that fundamentally transforms the consciousness of the human race, thus giving rise to decisive moments in its history?

Císařovský uses the motif of the horizon, dominated by the monument, and places the seemingly obvious silage pit into the context of mysterious prehistoric buildings as symbols of communication whose purpose is not known exactly, but which fundamentally affect our opportunity and capability for self-understanding. Communication with history and prehistoric artefacts is always asymmetric and enveloped in a haze of conjecture, more or less probable impressions and outright fabrications and fictions. No one knows exactly what truth history tells us, but we can be sure that what we are confronted with directly applies to us, our cults, and our status and our anchorage in nature and a world dominated by a mass-technology civilization. The silage pit is perhpas the best way of expressing such a confrontation!

Líbeznice clearly combines human prehistory with futuristic fiction, and thus presents *the past as the future* to us. Another picture is called *New Lány* and depicts windowless red-brick terraced houses fronted by geometrically composed building materials and piles of sand. The surrounding wasteland and emptiness is again dominated by a rich red sky. Yet this is not an image of an imminent universal apocalypse or a sketchy criticism of the devastated landscape and decline of housing culture. The construction materials around the new buildings are of key significance; their depiction here says that we cannot separate man and his dwellings from the technical process of exploiting natural energy and raw materials. Man operates technology to build a dwelling or to transport himself from one place to another, but the technology itself is not just a human creation. Ontologically speaking, borrowing from the above-mentioned Martin Heidegger, all technology is gathered together in *Gestell* as a means of "genuinely revealing everything as an exploitable condition".

In this world, even man and his labour energy is an exploitable reserve, hence in modern businesses the personnel department has slowly morphed into the "human resources" department. *New Lány* heralds an era of interchangeable structures without prospects, built by and dwelt in by "human resources", drawing on their own energy to use and reshape everything around them. When these resources are exhausted, the landscape is littered with their abandoned shacks, huts, caravans or iron structures. Sometimes, they even leave behind them dilapidated boards and propaganda signs cast in concrete, such as those which lined Czech roads during the Communist Normalization era in the 1970s and 1980s. There is still room for a sense of melancholy here, but not for beauty.

The reconstruction of the past and its intersection with the present permeates all of Tomáš Císařovský's work and is absolutely crucial even in his early conceptually historical project *From the Diary of My Grandfather the Legionnaire* from the late 1980s, in which images are organically complemented by words. It is also particularly noticeable in the *Stale Time* series, which is devoted to popular music in the Normalization era, in the *Without Their Horses* series, in which the living descendants of prominent Czech aristocratic families are portrayed in a civil atmosphere without pomp, and in a series of paraphrases of the pictorial themes of Socialist Realism, which originated in 2006 and 2007. Nor is it possible to forget the small but increasingly important *Power of Exception* series, in which the artist depicts controversial political leaders of the recent past, such as Gustáv Husák, Reinhard Heydrich and Emil Hácha.

Tomáš Císařovský, On the Way, 1988

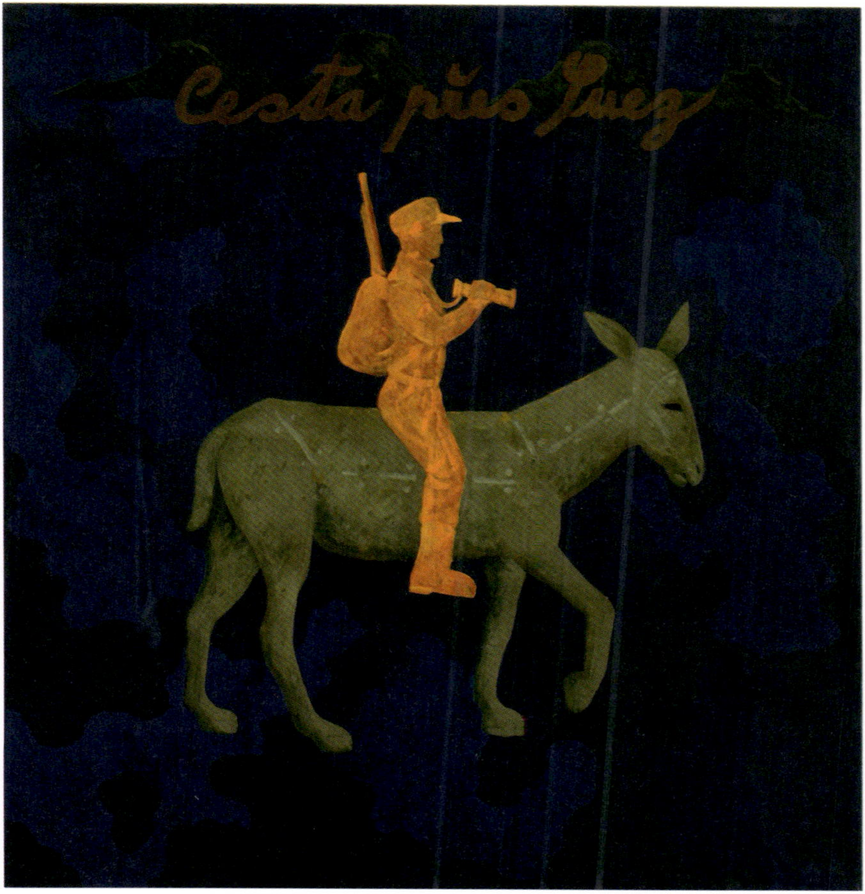
Cesta přes

It would be hard, for example, to find a more apt depiction of Communist Normalization than Císařovský's portrait of the "President of Forgetting", Gustáv Husák. On a bare, icy-white plain, the president stands dressed in an off-the-peg, shapeless winter coat, his fish eyes brimming with uncertainty. Only his hands betray his passion for smoking and hunting; in his left hand, he casually holds a cigarette, while in his right hand he clutches the ears of an oddly erect, petrified hare. All this is against a backdrop of concrete rings, those symbols of the emptiness of the Normalization era which, as they could not be stolen, were left scattered around many public areas in Czech towns and villages.

An extraordinary sensitivity to historical fabric and the ability to combine monumental history with the history of everyday life are manifested as early as the "legionnaire's diary" painting. War and the emergence of the republic are not just historical dates and events of high politics. The view of those who take part in them and who personally experience situations that we usually only know as passages in a textbook or as part of the general interpretation of our national history is equally important. Thanks to Císařovský's insight in the *Without Their Horses* series, for example, we see Count Kolowrat resting in a chair in his slippers, the Lobkowicz family posing more like a successful bourgeois family, and Prince Schwarzenberg paraded as an amusing eccentric.

This reconstruction of the past includes an emphasis on what makes any history history – the story. Císařovský insists on historical epicness and, by quite specific artistic means, constantly contrives more and more historical accounts which need to be listened to carefully. However, the names of the individual series are just as striking and important as the images that belong to them. The travel motif in the legionnaire grandfather series again clearly shows that history is always a path and an intellectual challenge, only at the end of which do we find the historical narrative. A grandfather's specific adventures and experiences of an expedition emerge from beneath the legionary myth. The question of the meaning of history constantly returns in all its inconsistency, urgency and difficulty; historical interpretations contradict each other and change over time.

Similarly, paraphrases of Socialist Realism are not intended to induce merely some sort of impression of historically ironic detachment, but, in contrast, introduce significant uncertainty into our seemingly unproblematic present. The proletarians portrayed by Císařovský at their machines or tools, whether a loom, turbine, masonry hammer, or file, are no caricatures of the official ideology of the time. On the contrary, they have their pride, perhaps because they lived in the last historical period in which work was considered a virtue, when the greeting was "Honour to Work!", and that ethic could not be debased even after it had been raped by Communist propaganda. What can our own era offer as something to honour? Total consumption, which has replaced the totalitarian illusion of a world of work?

The portraits of "Normalization celebrities" from the Stale Time series also have the remarkable ability to unnerve our seemingly banal and simple present. We can shudder with disgust at the "vampire" image of Pavel Liška or the "decrepit" duo of singers known as Kamélie, and chuckle at the "frolicsome" Václav Neckář, but when we view the historical picture in which, during the November 1989 revolutionary events, the national anthem is sung by the "Two Karels" – Kryl and Gott – we must feel the shivers running down our spine. Karel Kryl, an exiled folk-singer and symbol of resistance to the communist regime is now dead and buried, while Karel Gott, an icon of socialist pop-culture and symbol of collaboration, with that inimitable idiotic smile of his, has already become immortal in his own lifetime. But, then again, where are we ourselves and what have we actually been through in the past 20 years? What is normal and what is repulsive? When and how, in its impermanence, does ordinariness change and become a sign through which we understand ourselves and our history? And when and how does this sign of everyday life become a historical symbol?

Císařovský works with historicizing motifs with aplomb and finesse similar to the painter Antonín Střížek, from the same generation. This similarity aside, however, their creative methods are substantially different because, unlike Střížek's introspective paintings highlighting the purity of art forms, Císařovský's canvases always have more of a social tinge from the outset and are more straightforward in content. While Střížek emphasizes the time elapsed between the past and present, Císařovský always questions the historical meaning of the past

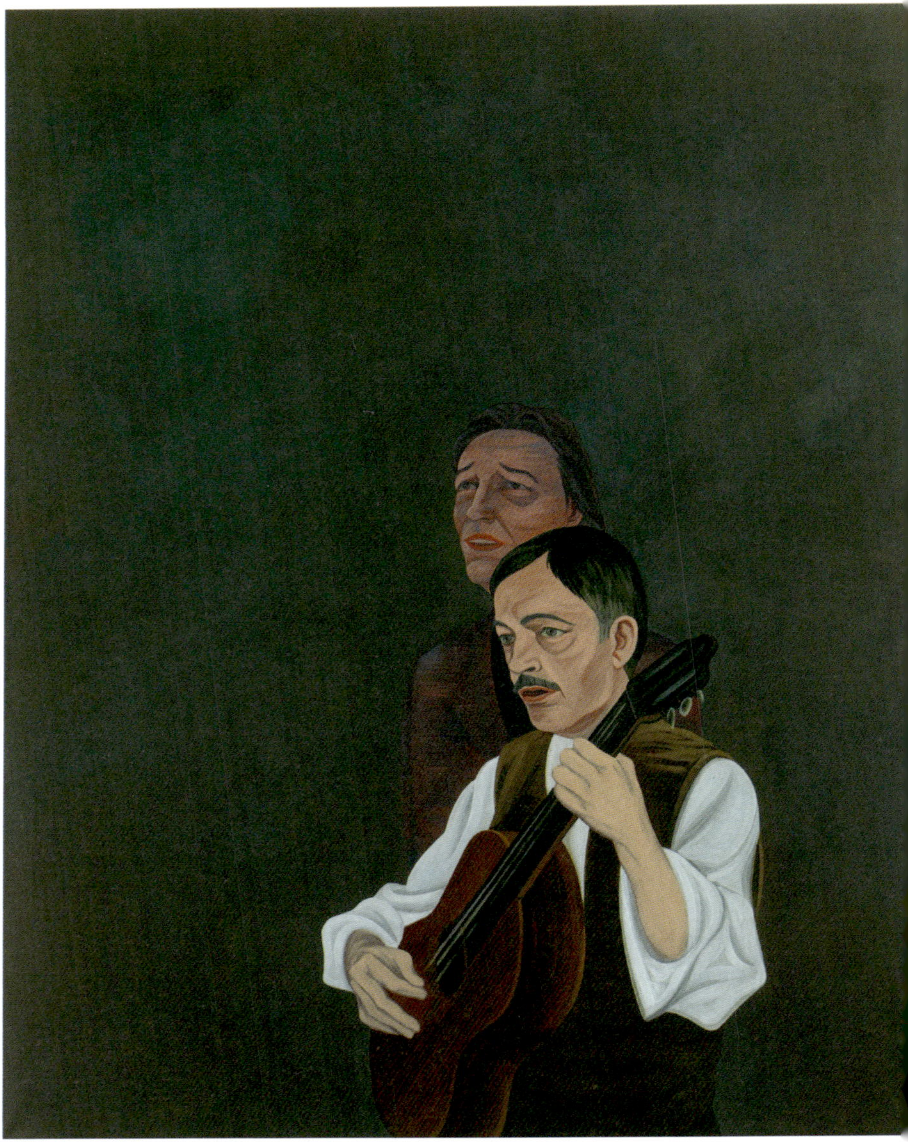

and offers his audience interpretations which, while possible, remain open.

The way he works with political themes is different from those artists who proceed by confrontation with prevailing political truths or who focus on the overall transgression and challenging of the political vision of the world. In contrast, Císařovský draws on commonly shared experiences and assumes that he is connected with his audience *a priori* by collective memory, which can take different forms – encompassing the memory of legionnaires, aristocrats, workers and Normalization. This memory and its associated feelings and experiences functions as a necessary form of pre-understanding, from which all possible critical meanings of the work are derived.

Císařovský is never interested in shallow social or political criticism, in which the artist uses art forms to communicate a "fundamental truth", such as that people should protect the environment, be considerate to each other or fight against oppression and despotism. Such truths are too flat and can only engender unproblematic consent in the viewer. If art is to be socially critical, it must create unrest and uncertainty and provoke the audience into constant questions about the meaning and content of the work. Indeed, evidence of this is can be found in the disturbing "civil canvases", to which Císařovský keeps returning over time and on which more or less indistinct characters in suits, for example, grab each other by the neck, are engrossed in their computers in a red desert, or communicate through animalistically sexual body language.

Císařovský undoubtedly uses socially conventional and seemingly simple signs and truths as an honest devotee of pop-art aesthetics emphasizing the banality of the world in which we live and how we express it. The themes depicted may therefore appear to be simple and unambiguous at first glance. After all, from the perspective of genre, what could be more conventional than, for example, a landscape or portrait? We are intimately familiar with the landscape and identify with it culturally and personally; it connects us with others and we are able to navigate and move around in it easily. It expresses a sense of common identity and shapes our collective memory. We understand it, we do not need to examine it further, and we feel comfortable in it because we have set it aside from nature as "our

Tomáš Císařovský, A Special Moment, 2003

view of the world". While it might mean something different for each of us, we share it, relate to it culturally and artistically as we would, perhaps, to poetry, a symphonic poem or a rural novel. Whereas nature is always foreign to us, forcing us to constantly study it, the landscape is ours, conjuring up in us familiar images and a sense of security, safety and home. Home is unthinkable without a landscape.

In the *Holidays in Bohemia* series, Císařovský respects the conventionally domesticated character of the Czech landscape, but also incorporates the creations of civilization, such as a silo, warehouse, production facility or factory, and displays them in their internal tension, condensation and inconsistency. The knocked-down structure of the spiral staircase found in any manufacturing plant thus dominates a flat field between Prague and Mělník and, paradoxically, gives a biomorphic impression. The clarity of the landscape gives way to the obscurity of civilization. While we are capable of understanding nature as our own landscape, the purpose of our ubiquitous and pervasive technology remains vague and open to us. In the middle of what appears to be self-evident and unproblematic, something emerges which is indisputably ours, but which we do not understand very well and which increasingly burdens not only us, but also originally alien nature.

Faced with such images of the Bohemian countryside, the viewer cannot automatically nod at some simple artistic message or social truth; rather, he must be actively involved in the interpretation of the work and use, as a guide, his memory, which forges a link between him and the artist.

In this context, I recall a conversation with one artist friend who, with a certain degree of exaggeration, called Tomáš Císařovský a "bourgeois artist". This was no prickly comment or desire to malign a colleague, which, given the total historical staleness of that phrase, would be rather foolish. But what was this colleague thinking of when he expressed that view? As it turned out, by using the adjective "bourgeois" he was highlighting the artist's ability to accommodate the general, or conventional, taste without having to pander or compromise himself. Besides relying on the general collective memory, Císařovský's work really does include methods of reproduction, illustration and decoration, which are the most common ways in which

Tomáš Císařovský, Karel Schwarzenberg, 1996

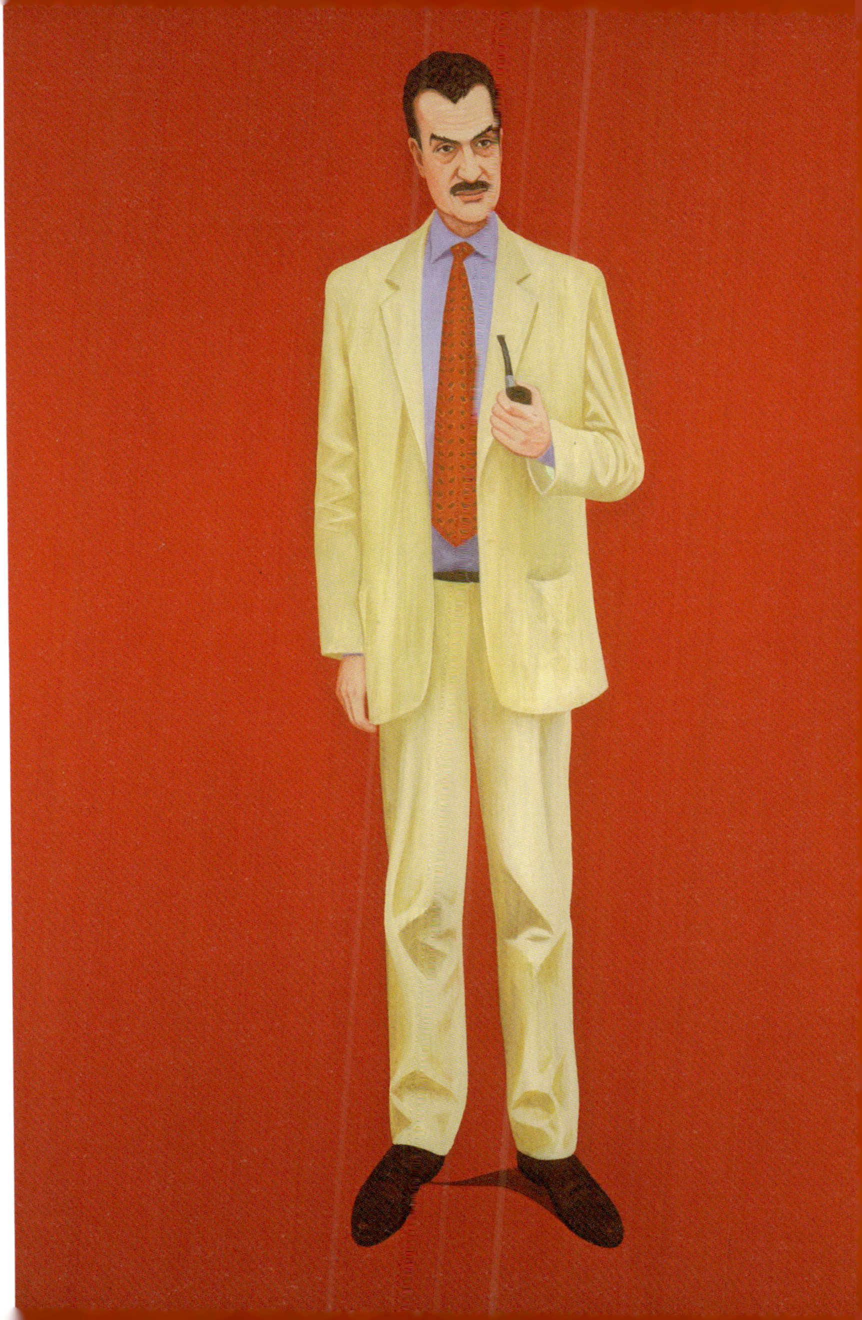

the consumer societies previously built up by the bourgeoisie now describe themselves. Yet it is precisely in these artistic methods that we find, for example, the imperishable charm and uniqueness of the visual cycle of American art collectors, as captured perfectly with bourgeois mannerisms in their homes and among the artefacts they owned by the British painter David Hockney in the 1970s and 1980s.

In 1983, the American philosopher Richard Rorty wrote an article, which, with his inimitable irony, he entitled "Postmodernist Bourgeois Liberalism". In it, among other things, he claims that conventions and anecdotes are a better means of resolving social conflicts and tensions than principles and metaphysical truths. Conventions here, however, do not mean the absolute pressure of society or the tyranny of the prevailing public opinion. They are not a manifestation of conformism, but an assumption of general understanding in a world of diverse opinion that is of limited validity and always only temporary. Bourgeois liberals defy the comfortable, but misguided stereotyping of the political right and left. According to Rorty, they are especially aware that their truths are never absolute, much like their constitutional freedoms and democratic culture, and therefore they prefer to proceed with prudence and attempt to reach a consensus. They are people with a strong sense of social justice and civil equality, yet, unlike radicals acting on principle, they believe that courtesy is not a weakness, but a virtue. Unlike conservatives, they do not blindly follow tradition; instead, they emphasize the human freedom to shape their own ideas of happiness and goodness and make decisions accordingly in their personal life.

In this respect, being a postmodern bourgeois liberal or artist is neither a slur nor an oxymoron. On the contrary, this designation is intended as an honest basis to understand the contemporary world with pragmatic modesty, knowledge of the limitations of one's own intellect and a healthy degree of cultural and historical scepticism. Looking at Císařovský's paintings, I am sure that this basis is present in them. In today's art, such a view constitutes, in itself, a special value because we never know if the diggers of our scientific and technological civilization, as they probe the overburden, will come across another Stonehenge, concrete piles similar to those rising in the Líbeznice field captured by Tomáš Císařovský's brush, or even a mysterious monolith changing the direction of our Space Odyssey.

ON YOUR MARKS!

POSTMODERN TRACES OF COLLECTIVE CONSCIOUSNESS IN THE WORK OF STANISLAV DIVIŠ

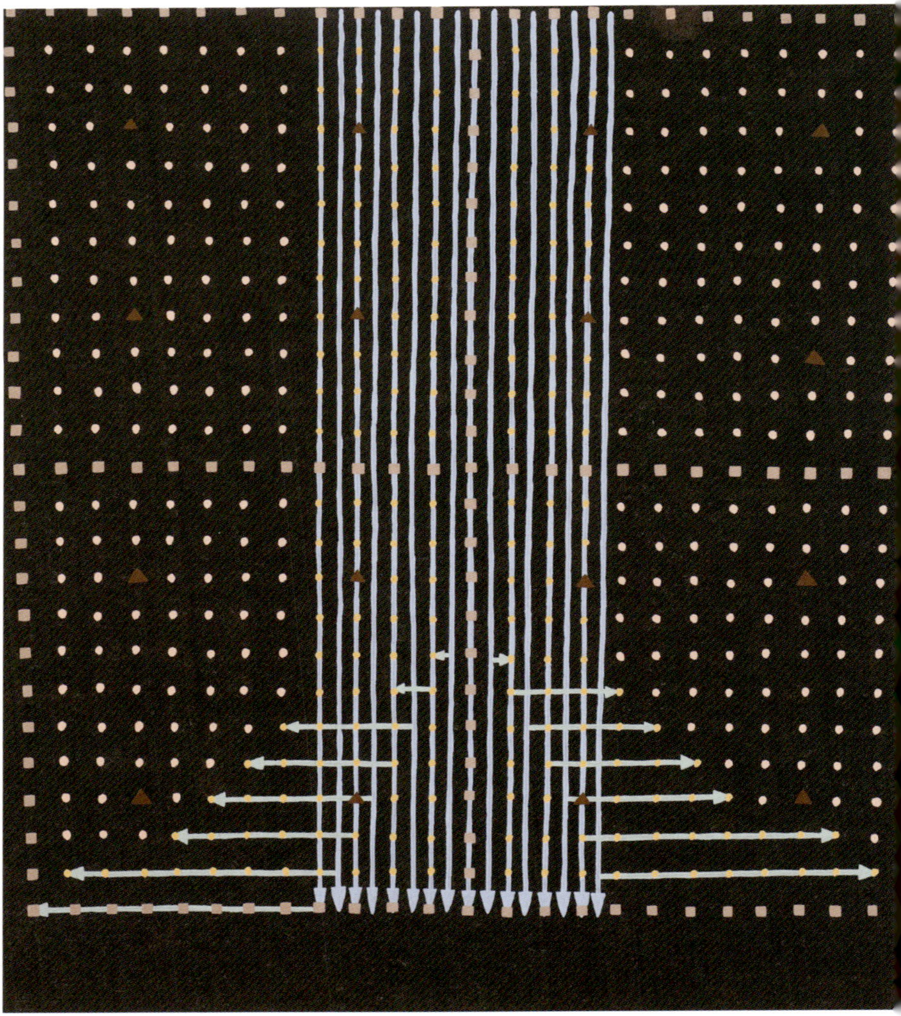

On Your Marks!

Postmodern Traces of Collective Consciousness in the Work of Stanislav Diviš

At the mention of Czech postmodern art, everyone is more than likely to recall the second half of the 1980s or the early 1990s and names associated in particular with the now legendary *Confrontations* exhibitions and the *Tvrdohlaví* (Heardheads) group. Postmodernism in the visual arts, however, did not develop in isolation. It was part of what is commonly referred to in sociology as collective consciousness. Such consciousness encompasses not only the cultural *Zeitgeist*, but also the value orientation, practical action and shared experience of certain groups or generations. As such, visual memories of *Confrontations* will forever be associated with memories of the *Pražská pětka* (Prague Five) theatre performances or new-wave rock music and minimalist compositions on the Czech and Hungarian experimental scene (primarily Agon in the Czech Republic and Group 180 with István Márta and Tibor Szemzö in Hungary).

This independent culture spread through inner courtyards, garages and suburbs, where the Communist regime, although it could still issue occasional prohibitions, was no longer able to completely control or to raze it as it had in the 1970s. Lengthy tram rides to the independent rock club Junior klub Na Chmelnici and the theatre Branické divadlo thus became a staple part of the collective consciousness of this shared culture. These were meeting points for those who had ripped up the social contract made during Normalization by the Communist elite and the citizens, which could be summed up as "We'll take care of politics, you take care of your weekend cottages!" And while the television screen was the domain of the crooner Karel Gott, Lucie Bílá and her playful song about her disobedient trainers, and good old Bohdalová's appearances in the Televarieté variety shows, in the suburbs a new restless and culturally starved generation was gathering which no one could bribe with a Skoda or a two-room flat in some high-rise.

Stanislav Diviš, Spartakiáda 90 no. 4, 1990

These days, Karel Gott is still warbling on the television, Lucie Bílá has become a cultural icon of the new regime, and reports on Bohdalová's antics are guaranteed Czech tabloid sellers. At first glance, it seems that, 20 years after the Velvet Revolution, Czech society is experiencing another Normalization era, this time in the illusion of civil liberties and cheap wealth produced by semi-legal capitalism and the corrupt political elite on both the right and left. Nevertheless, closer examination of the cultural field reveals clear fundamental differences. The old urban fringes have disappeared, but this is not a tragic loss because today's generation of hungry and restless can connect anywhere anytime via a laptop and share any culture. We live in an age in which the cultural periphery has been replaced by a terminal, and the information network has radically changed the functioning of the former centres of power. This makes it all the more interesting to see how the generation that created the cultural periphery in the 1980s has been transformed.

The artist and musician Stanislav Diviš was undoubtedly a mouthpiece of this generation as one of the organizers of the *Confrontations*, a member of the Tvrdohlaví art group, and as the frontman of *Krásné nové stroje* (Beautiful New Machines). As the singer of this group, which is still going, he once captured exactly the state of Czech society in Orwellian-dated timelessness, when, in the song Česká věc [The Czech Matter], in his unmistakably wild means of expression he sang a modified text by Jiří Olič: *I like compromises / they're like rat eggs / compromise is secured. / Weak as a fly, yet sitting / yesterday after we got together / on all fours finally / I burned with faith in the Czech matter.* By that time, no one had to torture us with hungry rats, as they did Winston Smith in Orwell's 1984, and unconditional love of Big Brother was not required. It was enough that we ourselves had assumed the behaviour of rats and considered it a matter worthy of national pride.

Diviš's canvases are dots, squares, crosses, circles, lines and vectors, sometimes supplemented by letters, numbers or other marks, organized into geometric shapes. The contrasts of the marks play to the equally important contrasts of the colours, but everything is very remote from abstract modernist painting and its "pure aesthetics" of shape, colour

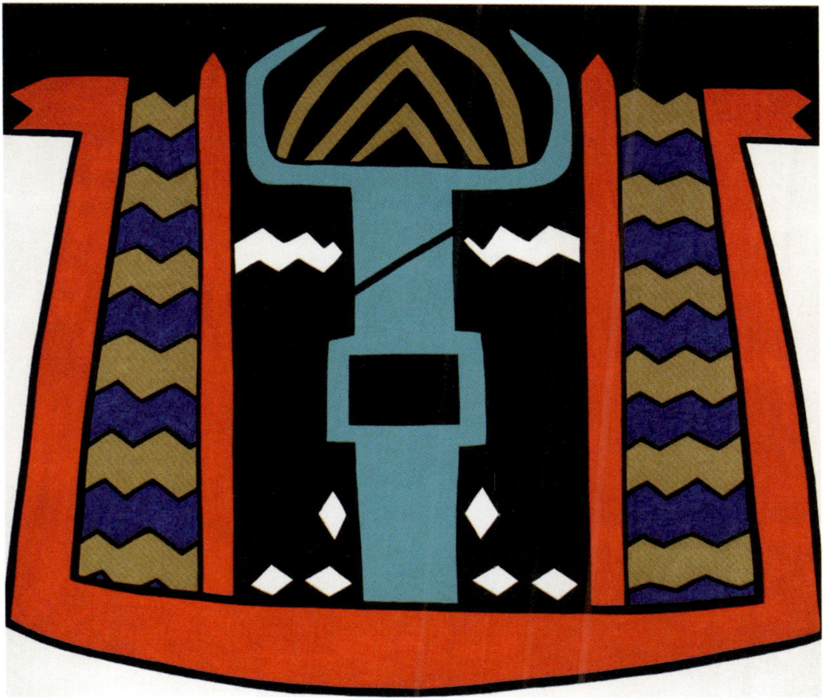

or composition. Stanislav Diviš generally draws on what has already been used or in some way established as a widely known and shared sign. He works with visual templates in the same way as he did with Olič's cited text for Krásné nové stroje, i.e. he always uses them "in his own image". As a result, fabric samplers from a long-abandoned textile factory in Aš serve as crucial inspiration for the *Remnants* series. The diagrams for Spartakiad sequences organized by the communist regime for the masses to demonstrate its physical strength and force, which were never realized after the regime's collapse in 1989, are the basis for the *Spartakiads* series. The *Two Worlds* series uses spontaneous childish drawings by the artist's son, Prokop; completely impersonal genetic tables, weather maps and instructional milking pictures also serve as

Stanislav Diviš, Ghost Ship, 1987

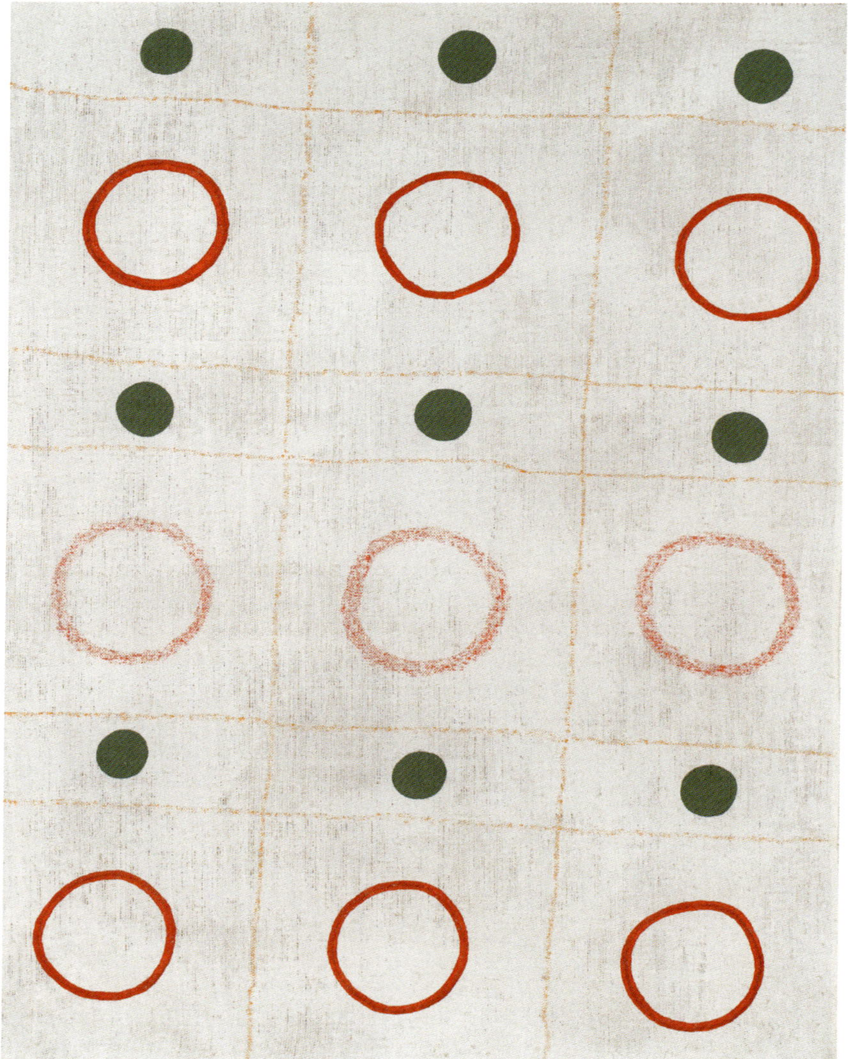

a template, model and inspiration. Furthermore, the artist frequently returns to individual themes, so each series is created over many years and is deliberately left open.

What is most notable about Stanislav Diviš's work is the method which the artist himself, with a strong dose of irony, dubbed "scientific realism" in the late 1980s. At the time, Communism considered itself to be scientific, while realism was socialist, so any unofficial combination of science and realism was a provocation. However, he was not just sneering at the official ideology, which by then no one took seriously, least of all those who, in its name, continued to persecute any sign of independent thought or art. Diviš's conceptual provocation actually need to be taken seriously, because his artistic method is based on exactness, comparison, transposition and aesthetic reduction of widely shared signs and entire semantic systems, as known for example from mythology, but also scientific tables, astronomical charts and geographical atlases.

When Kant's *Critique of Pure Reason* was published in 1781, our world was radically changed as modern thinking asserted itself with full force. The philosopher distinguished phenomena from things-in-themselves, which we may conceive, but never know. While the world has continued to hold onto its objective existence, our knowledge has become only the limited result of rational design. Reality is then what one creates with one's knowledge and organizes into sign systems.

Diviš is fascinated by this world of constant semantic structures and signs and returns to it to reconstruct and transform it into his own aesthetic system. Unlike the modernists, nevertheless, he does not create new imaginary worlds. He finds the desire to construct a new image and new man, an obsession of the modernists in their time, quite irksome. By the same token, however, Diviš does not approach artistic material with brazenly superficial deconstruction, resulting in the endless manipulation of original material and the interminable semantic game which trapped the careless and superficial readers of Jacques Derrida's philosophical texts.

In Diviš's work, we would search in vain for the arrogance of seekers of pure aesthetic expression and the frivolity of those who, in an effort

Stanislav Diviš, Musical Score no. 28, 1994

to attract momentary public interest, would exploit any theme or form. In many respects, his output resembles Borges's concept of an artistic work as something that is its own world in a world created by the artist or writer. A work is always more than output. The artist simply adds his skills to what was already here long before him. He is not seeking to express an original internal state of mind, but shared conventions, themes, language and other sign systems, which are the innermost essence of all art.

If any philosophical approach is close to Diviš, it is not so much Derrida's deconstruction as Foucault's "archaeology of knowledge". Diviš's canvases do not conceal some absolute undeniable reality as the basis of all "things". The signs do not lead to an immediate insight into the world, and therefore it is necessary to examine their mutual dependencies and their ability to define what is yet to be regarded as the world and its things. There is no choice between a thing and its sign, and therefore it is necessary to study the ability of signs to constitute our reality and to determine its scientific, cultural and historical canons. The natural world is conceivable only as a myth that is accessible to the human mind only through the mutual relations of symbols and characters.

What is striking about Diviš's paintings is the respect with which the author approaches the selected system of signs, whether mythological symbols, children's drawings, scores, fabric patterns or the diagrams for organized mass physical exercise events. As such, his work is genuinely reminiscent of the behaviour of an archaeologist who is trying to capture, as reliably as possible, original signs, their interactions and meaning. This "cleaning", however, is followed by a second phase in which the artefacts, arranged in this way, become the subject of aesthetic rendering, resulting in displacement of the meaning and the general "illumination" of the original sign system.

Instead of monstrous masses of bodies rolling through the gates of Strahov Stadium and spilling into various shapes in this huge area, only individual signs and outlines of the movement of human masses appear in Diviš's images. Here, the essence lies not so much in the ideology, in the name of which thousands of people obeyed the command "On your marks!" and, with discipline, regaled the audience with a spectacular show of the geometric patterns and colours of a marshalled throng in motion. Diviš is not superficially questioning the political context of the Spartakiads, but casts his keen eye much further, focusing on the actual physical or material nature of our aesthetic intoxication.

The *Spartakiads* cycle is undoubtedly an aesthetic reduction of the original images of manipulated and rehearsed human bodies, in which the question of the aesthetic instincts of man and his ability to create a cohesive system out of any activity is encoded. So it is with the *Scores* cycle, in which Diviš the artist is most closely aligned with Diviš the musician. Here, too, the transposition of a musical record eventually displays a system of signs, the ultimate purpose of which is something as fundamentally unportrayable as music. Whereas Orphists such as František Kupka and, after them, Trevor Bell and others, wanted to convert music into images, through his cycle Diviš is telling us, among other things, that this artistic path is a dead end because it is possible to depict only the sign system opening up the way to music.

While the impetuous interpreters of Derrida's philosophy create according to the stupidly sloganistic template "Deconstruction, not Reconstruction!", Diviš resolves to engage in any aesthetic deconstruction only after a thorough examination of the purpose of the original material with which he is working. This purpose must also be present and preserved in the new work, despite any loose paraphrasing, fragmentation or reduction.

This two-stage approach is perhaps most noticeable in the *Two Worlds* cycle, in which the artist draws on the childishly ungainly drawings of his son. We are all familiar with similar drawings from our own childhood or by our own children. The artistic skills of us adults have also often remained quite stunted, so they are not much different from children's drawings. Even in this cycle, however, Diviš does not aim to capture the authentic expression of the "pure" soul of a child; first and foremost, he is probing the possibilities and ways in which the child's view of the world is formed, what his ties are to the world of adults, and what transitions and transformations may occur, for example, on the father–son axis.

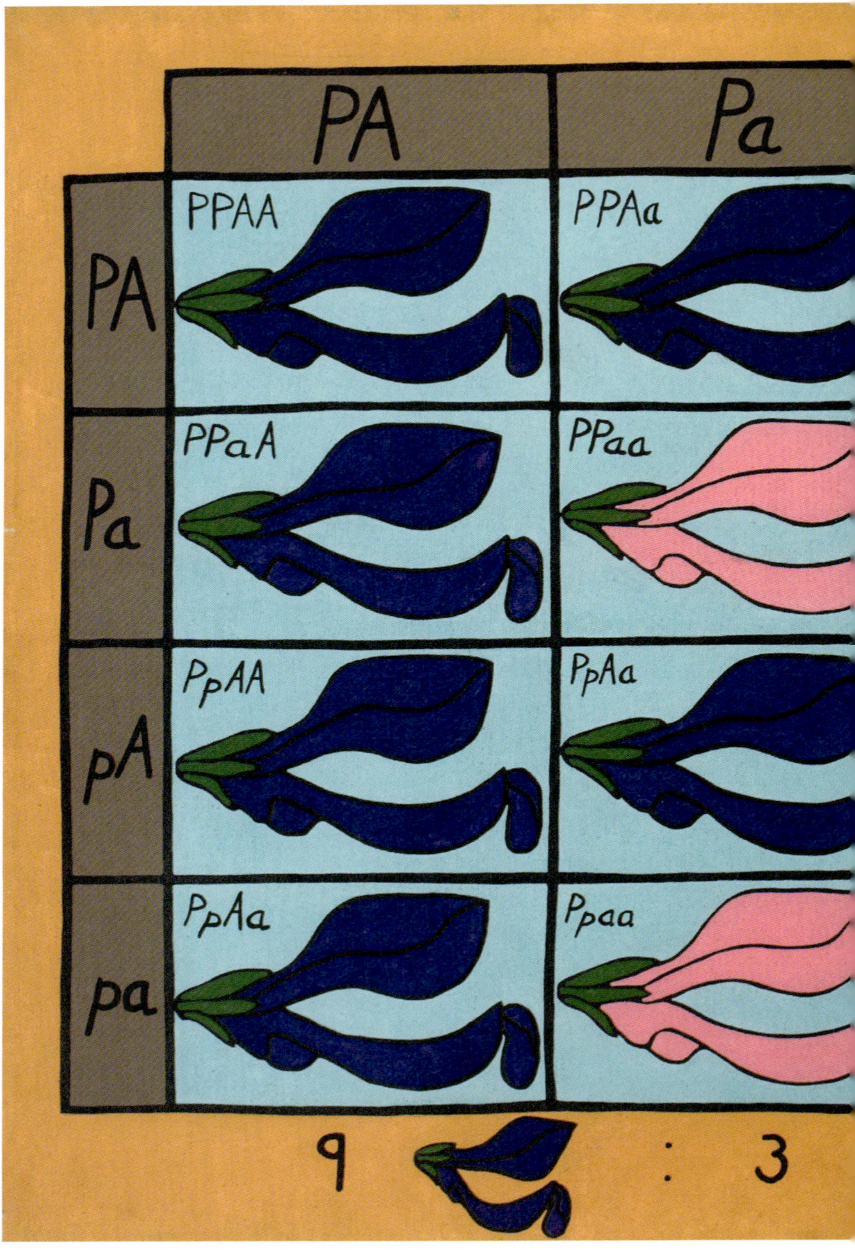
PA
Pa
PA
Pa
pA
pa
PPAA
PPAa
PPaA
PPaa
PpAA
PpAa
PpAa
Ppaa
9
:
3

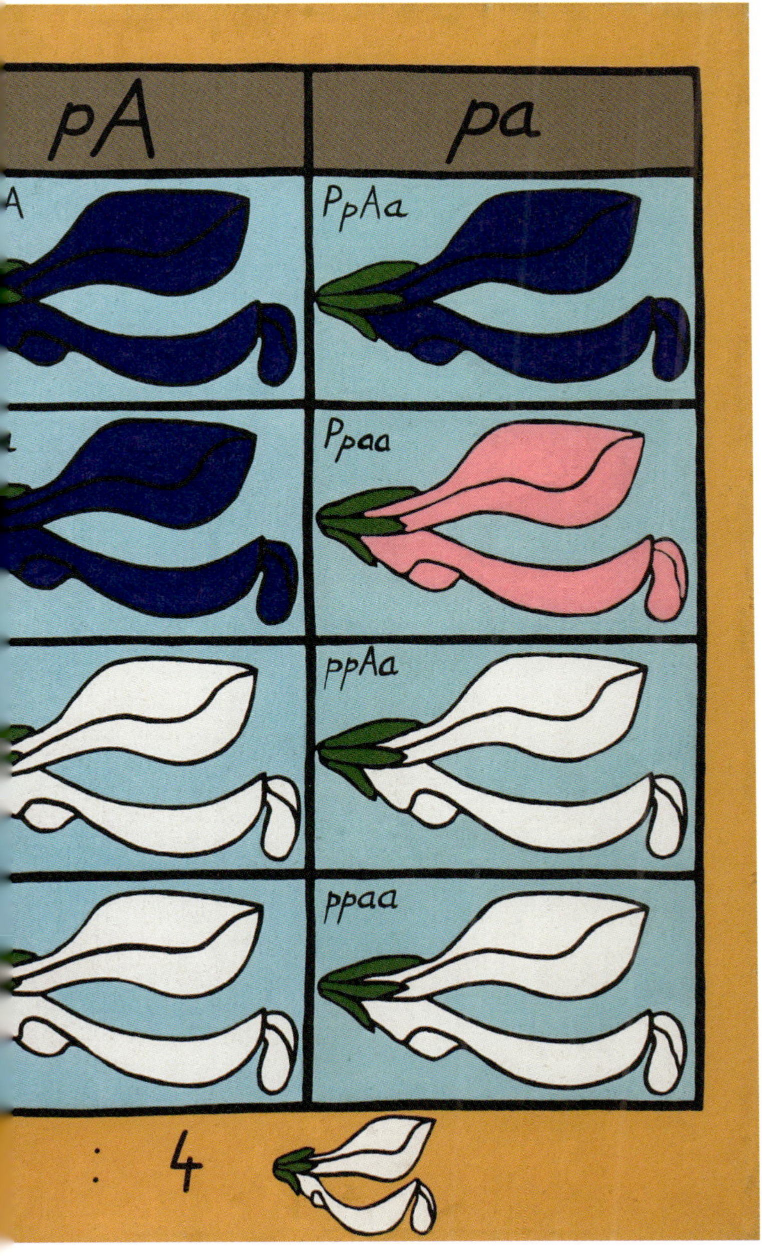

Stanislav Diviš, Salvia Viridis, 1998

The themes, whether taken from advertisements or comics, are just as important as the drawing itself. The painter transmits it to a canvas, moving and, above all, radically transforming it by means of the colour composition. A children's bike, scary monsters or Ferda the Ant with his friend Baggins the Beetle in "new colours" radiate not only the pencil strokes of a child, but also the painter's effort to bring together comedy and seriousness, cultural and biological continuity and discontinuity, and admiration and irony. The two figures drawn by little Prokop in the light of a lamp become, after the adult intervention of big Stanislav, *Night Walkers* and the child's world suddenly finds itself in one of the

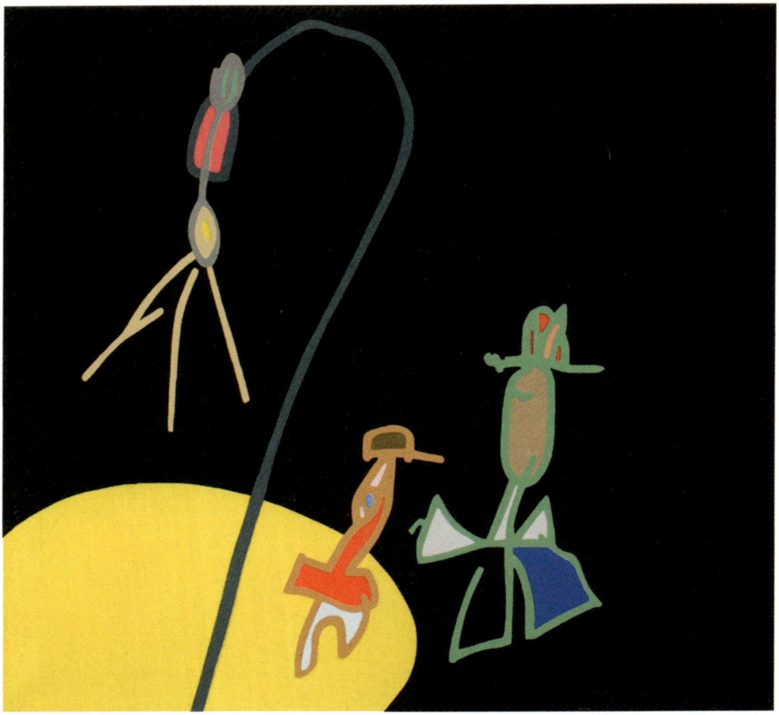

Stanislav Diviš, Two Worlds (Nightwalker) no 50, 2001

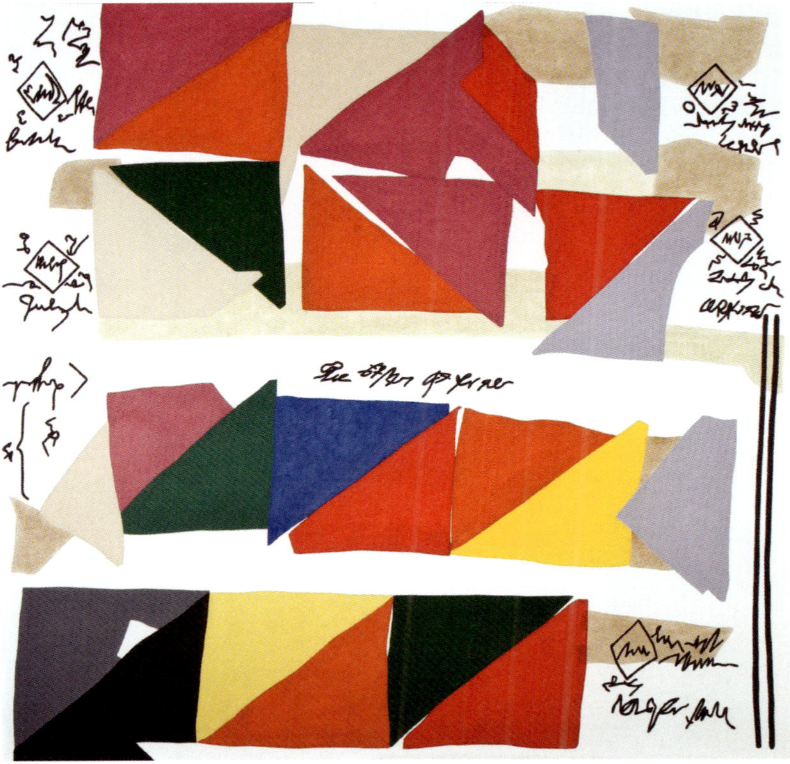

classic themes of Czech modernism as we know it from the paintings of Josef Čapek and František Hudeček, as well as the poems of Jiří Kolář and Vítězslav Nezval and the theoretical studies of Jindřich Chalupecký. And the childishly classic characters of Ferdy the Ant and Baggins the Beetle undergo a similar radical transformation on a grotesque-laden canvas with the ironically pathetic subtitle *A Czech Trio*.

Stanislav Diviš, Remnants no. 26, 2009

Although the work of Stanislav Diviš is cited today as a typical example of Czech postmodernism, it must be stressed that his is a very peculiar combination of aesthetic freedom, abstraction and sceptical realism that has given up on the possibility of capturing the immediate world and life in its unreduced authenticity. It incorporates the experience that our reality is always dependent on expression, whether artistic, mythological, scientific, craft or gymnastic expression. Like Borges's stories, Diviš's images constantly remind us that we cannot get to the world directly, but only through stories or images in which other images and stories are already present, which themselves undoubtedly contain traces of other stories, images and symbols...

ART AS POLITICAL AN-AESTHETICS

THE COURAGE AND ART OF JIŘÍ DAVID

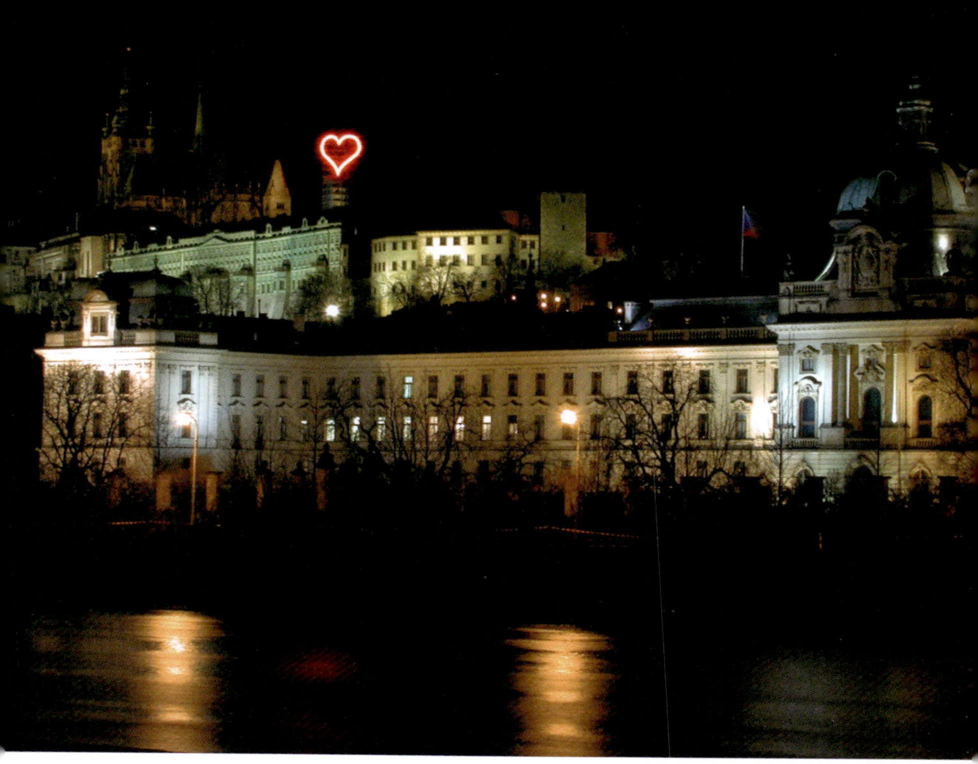

Art as Political An-aesthetics

The Courage and Art of Jiří David

Every encounter with my friend Jiří David is an adventure. I never know in advance what exactly is on his mind, what he is working on, who he has picked an argument with, what has caught his eye or what he is personally involved in. He is combative and thoughtful, unusually critical and enthusiastic, explosive and generous. What others keep to themselves, he has to keep disclosing at exhibitions, in newspapers, television interviews, manifestos, petitions, and even at political demonstrations. He causes a stir because of the way, unlike the majority of Czech artists, he is political, and public and intimate themes or topics are always combined in his works. He is an example of an increasingly rare activist artist who is still convinced of the need to defend a common space for public discussion and criticism of the powerful in this digitally fragmented and shattered time.

In Czech culture, there has been this idea for two centuries that the artist is the conscience of the nation and therefore must criticize politics from the position of higher moral principles. We adopted the erroneous view from the German Romantics that culture is something higher, while politics is an inherently base activity that needs to be constantly "inspired". In such conditions, however, rather than critical political art, it is possible to create only a vague cultural critique of politics, as a rule full of general rhetoric and empty moralistic phrases. The result is fatalism or aestheticism, those two curses of Central European culture.

In contrast, Jiří David's work has always been determined by aesthetic and civic courage. At the end of the 1980s, for example, David's series *Home* (1988) and *The Czech Dream* (1989) launched a new game in Czech art with motifs and symbols that had been used thousands of times and were often even tiresome. The lettering and decorative twigs on the notice boards of socialist labour brigades, minimalistically depicted yet decoratively embellished national maps, tricolours against a background of pink flowers, painted fairground

Jiří David, Neon Heart, Prague Castle, 2003 (photo: Jan Mahr)

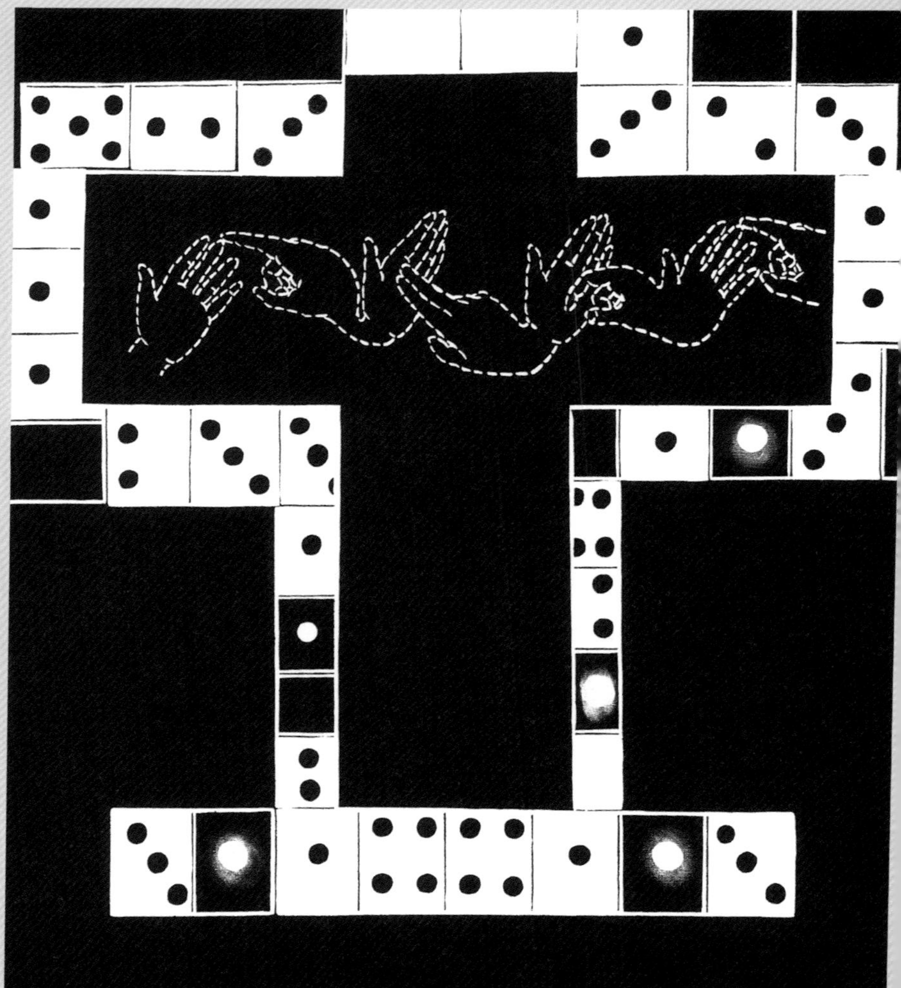

hearts, and images of girls in folk costumes, all this still suggests that, at that time, the changes in the political regime were accompanied by gradual changes in general thinking and thus in the aesthetic code that we have come to label Czech artistic postmodernism.

Jiří David reassembled traditional symbols of Czechoslovak statehood and folklore art, completely worn out by Communism, in order to interpret them in a new light and restore their capacity for symbolic, i.e. open, understanding. Marcel Duchamp, by enabling even the most ordinary object to become art, substantially hampered the work of all future artists. Since then, the artist's ability to recognize new poetry and symbolism in everyday reality and recount it to the audience has become much more important. Duchamp's *readymades* do not imply that everything is art, but something rather different, namely that everything can become art. As, after Duchamp, Joseph Beuys very astutely recognized, it is up to the artist how to deal with this task and which objects to choose for his or her symbolic language.

For Jiří David, it is significant that, at the end of the 1980s, he chose symbols which had been manipulated by the official propaganda, imposing on them a narrow ideological interpretation and using them to exploit the collective consciousness of society at the time. He was attracted by the thought of entering the world of the expressive forms of the decaying Communist regime which, during Normalization of the 1970s and 1980s, had gradually lost the ability of self-understanding and self-perception. The vocabulary and iconography of Communist ideology lost all meaning and only served to maintain official rituals rather than violently enforce the totalitarian world view of society as a whole.

As we know from the general systems theory, without the ability to understand and describe its actual operation, each system loses its ability to develop, and is therefore doomed. Yet few believed in the rapid demise of the Communist system at this time; most people were generally content with problem-free survival in the middle stream of the increasingly rotting, although now seldom bloody, river of real socialism. One of the few exceptions was individuals and groups from various fields of alternative art who, in the 1980s, found themselves

Jiří David, INRI, 1987

able to work outside the official scene without being herded into the claustrophobic ghetto of the parallel dissident culture.

In this political and social constellation, Jiří David decided, in his pictorial series *Home* and *The Czech Dream*, to combine the work of a cultural anthropologist, uncovering various historical and social layers of meanings and uses of specific signs, with the committed attitude of someone asking whether those signs can have meaning and significance for the present, and if so what it is, and whether the systematic use of official ideology has been totally depleted. The artist analysed various forms of the pragmatic use of national or popular symbols, reconstituted their iconic imagery and, in this particular combination of a historicizing and contemporary approach, eventually asked a much more general question about the free flitting of signs in our semantic landscape. At the same time, he never ceased to wonder how such flitting affects politics, how propagandistic arsenals of words, icons and symbols were created, and, in this respect, in what areas the committed artist should therefore direct his flights and expeditions.

Jiří David is well aware of the fact that, in the wake of the modernist avant-garde era, art can only be symbolic. Whereas, in the 1990s, he examined not only visual forms of religious or mystical symbols, but also, for example, sign language, when President Havel left office in the winter of 2003 David installed a neon heart on the Basilica of St George in the Castle complex, causing a commotion that resulted in parliamentary interventions. Upon seeing the panorama of Prague Castle illuminated in this way, the outraged citizens believed this confirmed their conviction that "there are brothels everywhere now, even at the Castle".

In contrast, however, the younger generation of artists immediately and precisely understood the meaning of the whole project and participated in it by shading the left part of the heart so that the Castle was illuminated by a red neon question mark for some time. The semantic game with the neon heart over the panorama of the traditional seat of Bohemian kings and Czech presidents thus became much closer to written and spoken language. Linguistic and visual expression became interconnected, further intensifying the nervous

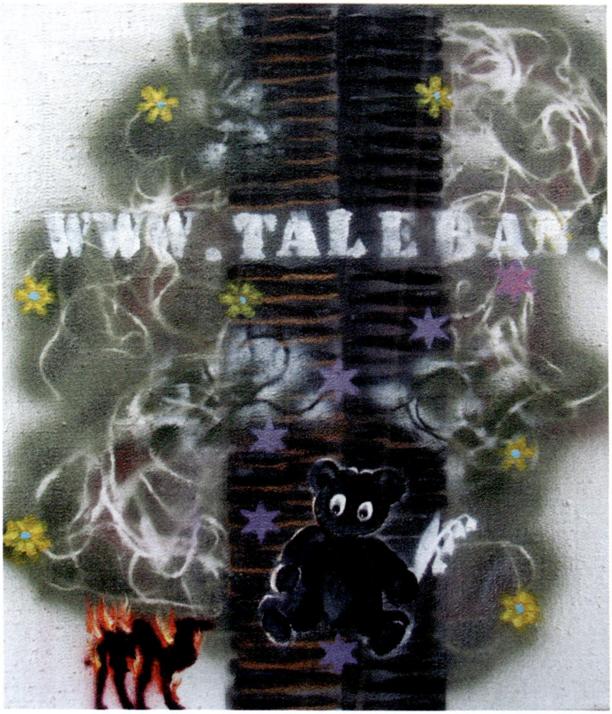

mood in a society already perplexed about what was happening to the appearance of the focal point of the history and present of the Czech Lands. Who would be the next lord of Prague Castle? Who would he bring with him and where would he take the Czech Lands? At the time when Havel was leaving presidential office and before a new president had been elected, these and other questions were only natural, and the neon heart/question mark radiated them into the freezing winter nights.

Differentiation and transgression, two critical methods of contemporary art, were borrowed from Jiří David by his younger colleagues, and so, at the turn of the millennium, the whole of that red

Jiří David, www.taleban.com, 2001

glow over Prague might have reminded us that artists should not be the conscience of the nation. They should be rebels who smash cultural stereotypes and rigid images of collective memory, and who loudly voice generally uncomfortable or even unacceptable questions.

The artist behind the neon heart could have been irritated by his younger colleagues because they had radically intervened in his work. Jiří David, however, did not condemn the "intrusion" on his artefact as a case of violence against art or even cultural vandalism. He, too, believes that art is always also a social conflict and controversy about who is fit to interpret a particular artefact and how, and thus convey its social understanding. And in this conflict it is possible to parasitize other people's art and even cultural or social goods of all kinds.

However, few understood this at the time, and the whole debate again became mired in the usual clichés and ineradicable reflections on how our present time is culturally superficial, socially rotten and decadent if officials permit the installation of a red neon heart on a historically sacred site of the Czech nation and the symbol of Czech statehood and the homeland. In the spirit of bitter political romanticism, a large part of Czech society, including its political and cultural elite, still expects artists to produce works confirming the general cultural canon and the established visions of our collective identity. Here, the Castle district (Hradčany, or, more pedantically, Hradčana) plays an absolutely prominent role, so any independent interpretation of a universally accepted iconic image or any manipulation which might in any way call it into question or transform it into something other than its own image is considered to be cultural sacrilege.

David's work provokes heated discussion; the artist is regularly accused of exhibitionism, superficiality, searching for cheap popularity or tracking fashion trends and sticking to the surface of even the most superficial media reality. According to established ideas, art should *beautify* reality, not *problematize* it. Resistance to experiments, praise of mediocrity and the easy life as the "idyll", in the full abomination of this (in Czech) verbal diminutive, are fundamental features of Czech culture, which David does not respect and against which he rails more or less subversively.

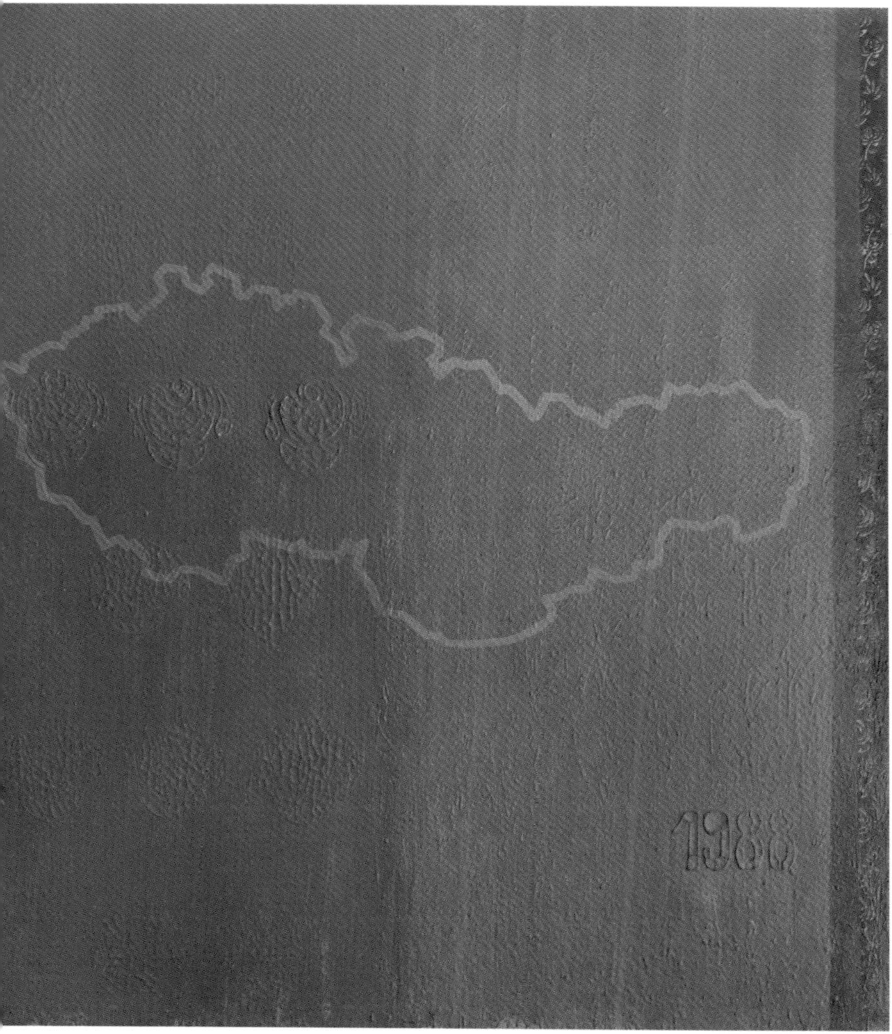
1988

However, Jiří David is no superficial provocateur keen to cause a scandal at any cost. In these times, constantly flooded with the most wide-ranging excesses, ultimately the greatest provocation is to remain completely normal. For this to be possible, we must first ask ourselves the most provocative and most impossible question of all, which is what it means to be normal.

The main device in David's work is not the question "What is worth doing in contemporary art?" but "What is still valid in contemporary art?" The problem of authorship and authenticity, or the problem of the basic conditions of modern art, is addressed by Jiří David as follows: *authenticity is not a prerequisite for the creation of a work, but a part of its internal structure.* Unlike the classically postmodern "death of the author", along with the "death of the subject" and the "death of man", which in the last twenty years have become an unbearable cliché of cultural snobs and coffeehouse chatterers, David considers the issue of the authorship of a work to be entirely legitimate and constantly returns to it. Yet he diverges from the modernist canon by using authenticity as a cipher rather than as the default artistic gesture. A cipher incorporating not only the life, body, motives and doubts of the artist, but also the lives of his nearest and dearest, i.e. his wife and children, of whom his son Daniel in particular was often a subversive object and subject of David's paintings and photographs.

Perhaps most striking is the creative method in the 2005 image *Biography*, where, against a background of biographical and personal data written in block letters, stands the artist's helplessly naked figure. This image must, literally, be read, so we discover that Jiří David is 189 cm tall, no longer writes letters, sometimes has bad breath and, apart from flies in the summer, is not really into killing other living beings. The writing exercises familiar to us from primary school are given a visual and very intimate dimension here, so that, in the picture, the author exposes himself to the viewer both literally and figuratively.

This self-portrait creates a new symbiosis between the visual and literary arts, in which, however, the person of the artist/author remains central. Like Michel Montaigne in his essays, in which sceptical considerations about the inconsistencies of our world and thoughts are accompanied, for example, by passages on the philosopher's digestive problems, Jiří David is also able to combine the patent with what remains latent, and the banal with what is important and significant. Indeed, in Montaigne's light style and witty aphorisms, many saw only superficiality and dilettantism, i.e. vices similar to those of which David is accused. In these criticisms of seemingly light and pompous comments on diverse ideas, moods, feelings and sensations, one important feature of modern culture, namely that neither thought nor art has any sense without personal insight, is lost.

The way David works with the problem of authenticity indicates another feature of his work which often triggers sharp negative reactions: his social conditionality. While stereotypical ideas tempt us to regard the artist as someone who communes with the absolute all the time, David's work is obviously social, always responds quickly to what is happening in the here and now, and is not afraid of its own impermanence. The artistic point of departure is not metaphysics, but society in its continuous transformations.

David, however, is intuitively very well aware that modern-day *society* is itself a *metaphysical problem*. Nevertheless, modern philosophy is unimaginable without social sciences or linguistics. We speak of the "linguistic turn" or the "priority of democracy over philosophy", and philosophers translate philosophical problems as "social issues". Similarly, David constantly filters individual visual forms from their social context in order to transform them and then return them where they belong, i.e. in society in its immediate mood and momentary forms of communication.

Yet Czech culture has a strong tendency to suppress all social problems and replace them with the idyll of friendship and solidarity overcoming the hardships and dangers of the world which is somewhere out there, but is not "ours". Hardly surprisingly, through his constant problematizing of and commenting on social reality, David has, in a way, alienated himself from the Czech environment, and his work becomes comprehensible only in an international context.

Jiří David is exceptionally sensitive to what has not yet surfaced in society and, for the time being, manifests itself only by the force of the undercurrent. What we others still see as a blur, the artist is already

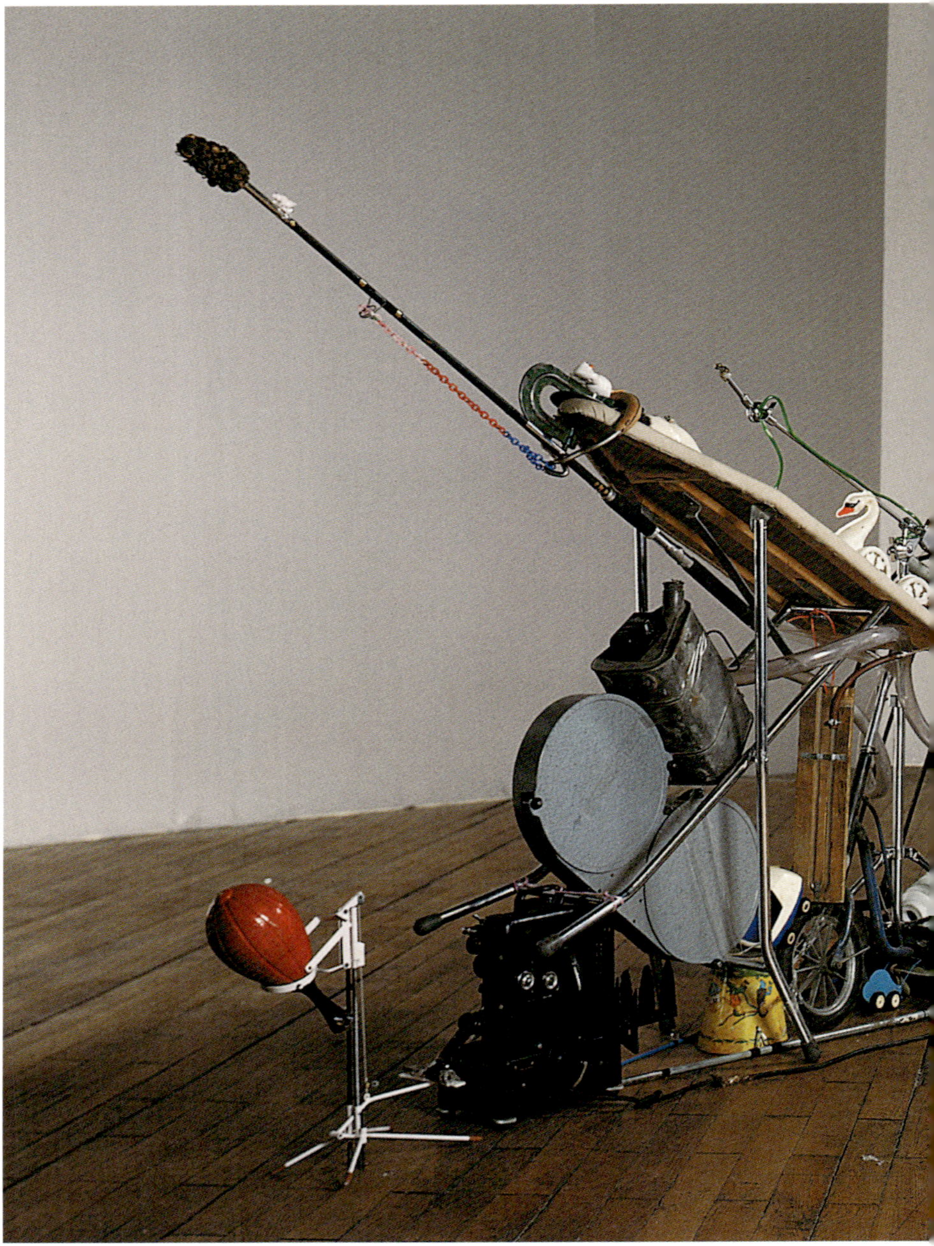

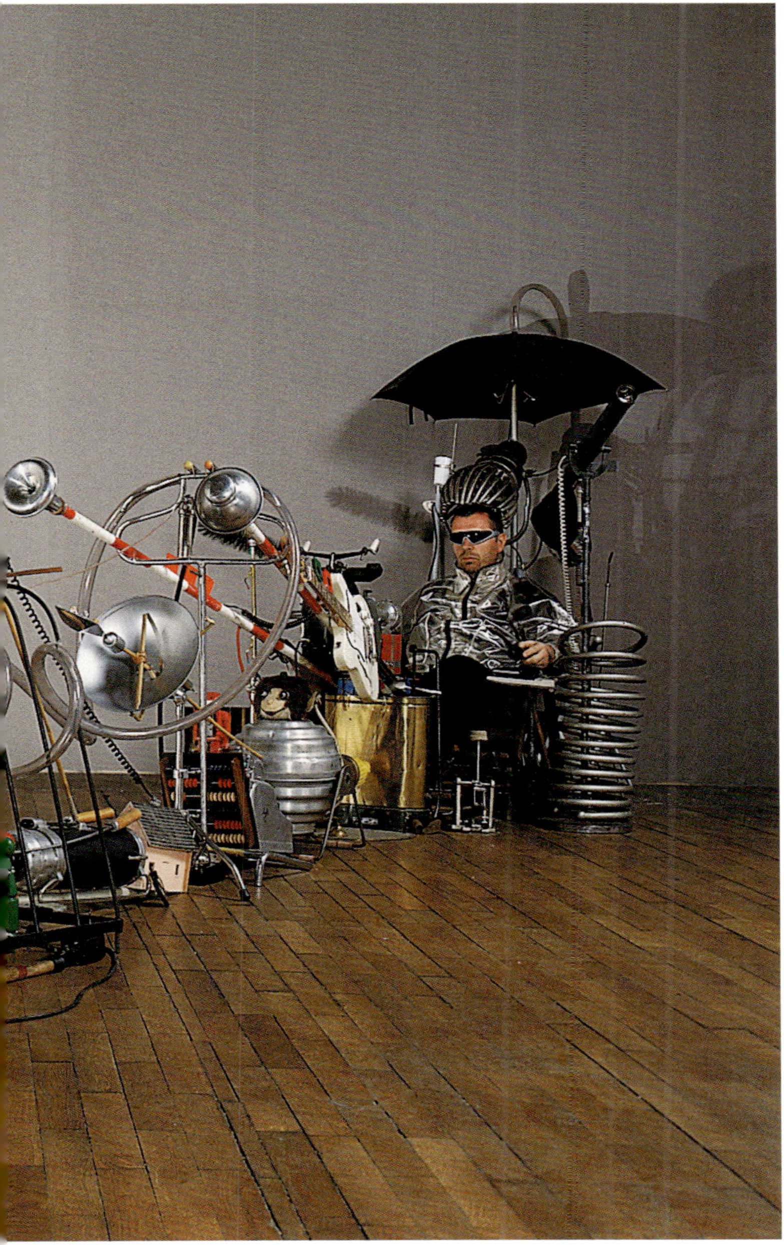

Jiří David, Rocket – Level 3, 1999

able to give a clear visual form. Unlike the "Vorsprung durch Technik", or advancement through technology, boasted by German automotive engineers, here we are faced with artistic "advancement through intuition", which, in hindsight, we often fail to realize, but which, in its time, radically influences the themes and forms of artistic expression.

This ability to capture the pulse of the moment could, of course, turn against the artist at any time, as we saw in August 2001 when, fascinated by the fundamentalist Taliban movement and its strict prohibitions in the visual sphere, David painted the notoriously symbolist picture "Taliban.com", whose vertical axis is determined by two cartridge belts which, in the upper third, are intersected with the sprayed title of the painting. After Bin Laden's attack on New York three weeks later, the semantic richness of the image collapsed along with the towers of the World Trade Centre – the political situation and media presentation of the subsequent "war on terror" in this case literally steamrolled the artwork by the force of their own iconography.

A more "fortunate" case of the social resonance of a work of art is undoubtedly one of the highlights of David's output, namely the series *My Hostages* (1998), in which characters dressed in costumes from children's games and fairy tales have their hands tied and a sack thrown over their head. At a time when we were just starting to talk about paedophilic violence and there was still no moral panic in matters of the sexual protection of children, David reminded us, with disturbing images of bound children, that torture and sadism are not hidden behind the walls of concentration camps and prisons, but are spread out in our minds and haunt us in our homes. Violence can be obvious or hidden and may take the form of tape or rope, or just as easily Mickey Mouse trousers or "funny" masks. The childhood idyll also includes a repressed form of violence. Long before the images of tortured prisoners from the American-managed prison in Abu Ghraib, we were able to corroborate here that the most effective way to rid a victim of his humanity is to cover his face. Looking at a victim's face could cause an undesirable flicker of humanity in the torturers.

Jiří David is not the type of intellectual artist who would construct his visual works to the very last detail in advance and base them on

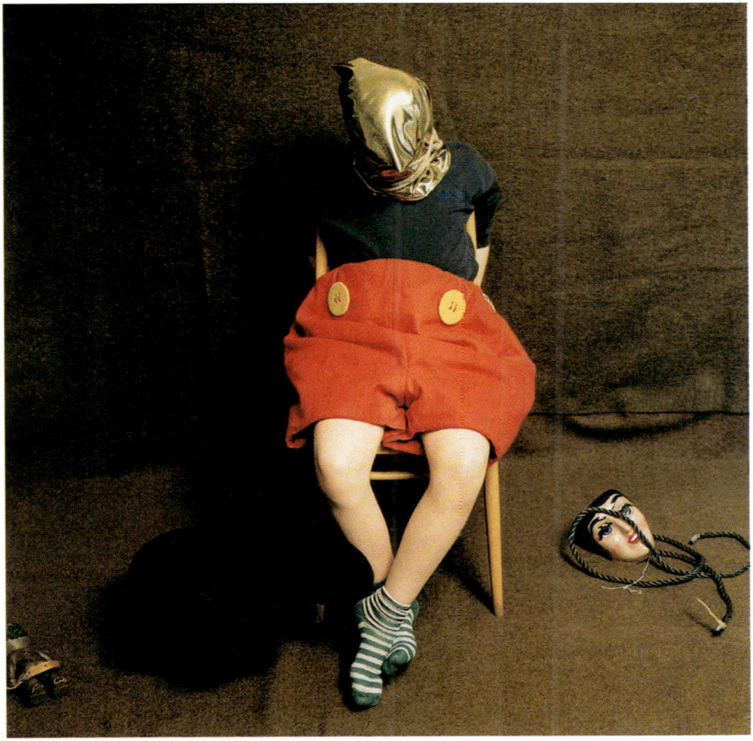

contemporary art theory. His work is radically intuitive, but this enables him to capture images of our ever more alarming and disunited world with all the more persuasiveness and accuracy. Similarly, another of David's internationally known series, *No Compassion* (2002), combines the simplicity of the original idea, technical clarity, and creative originality, which opens up the work to many varied, but contextually well-defined, interpretations.

It would be hard to find more banal pictures in the world today than portraits of world leaders, terrorists and religious leaders. Art is thus infused with something that is originally the opposite – politics

Jiří David, from the series My Hostages , 1998

and its rigid iconography. If the artist then inserts tears into these portraits, he breaks the iconography in the most radical way: a tear is not only improper, in that "politicians don't cry", but is also often the consequence of the grossest political propaganda and manipulation. While we can argue whether they are tears of true or false emotion, we will never know the exact answer and it is not important. What is important is that an artistic installation here can "freeze" the manipulative effects of political iconography in today's media consumer society: *the aesthetic code works as political an-aesthetics.*

We live in a time when there is no point in constantly debating whether this era is kitschy and therefore morally defective. If everything can be art, then everything can, naturally, be kitsch. The only way to resist such a world is to continuously nurture doubt about what appears to look like the solid and unquestionable foundation of our world. And we can only doubt if we think about the apparent confines of the world. Descartes was well aware of this, but now the burden of philosophers must also be borne by artists.

Jiří David has an extraordinary talent to capture and destroy the very images in which today's modern global civilization is eager to confirm the apparent certainties and truths about itself. The sense of visual symbolism in his works is simultaneously accompanied by a capacity for sociological or political abridgement. He is constantly trying out more and more techniques, experimenting with new symbols and returning to old ones in order to define for himself what is still important and what is not. Metaphorically speaking, he always thinks and creates on the road, not at home in the safety of generally shared ideas.

DIALOGUES OF A CHILD AND INVENTOR

THE RENAISSANCE TALENTS OF PETR NIKL

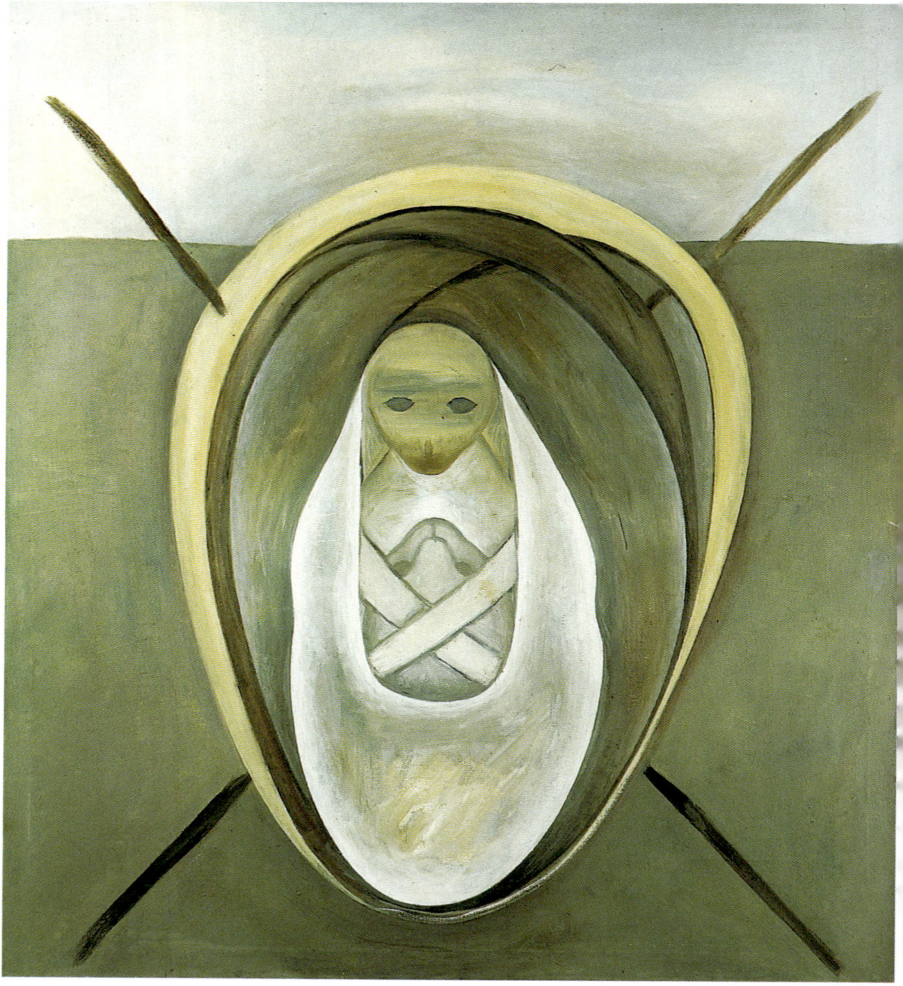

Dialogues of a Child and Inventor

The Renaissance Talents of Petr Nikl

Publishing *Lives of the Most Excellent Painters, Sculptors, and Architects*, Giorgio Vasari founded the modern history and theory of art and the cult of the artist as a social and cultural star. The artistic mission was thereafter nothing less than to correct the deficiencies of nature by a perfect brushstroke, pencil sketch or chisel movement. This mission required not only the relevant skills, but also knowledge in the fields of mathematics, physics or medicine, which budding artists were expected to acquire in a special educational institution – Florence's Accademia delle Arti del Disegno, which was founded at Vasari's instigation in 1563.

It was at this point that the figure of the Renaissance artist was born, equipped with skill and education, a rational calculus and original genius, technical discipline and free imagination, as well as social prestige and personal vanity or conceit. That is why Vasari's *Lives* includes many anecdotes, one of the most famous of which relates to Michelangelo's visit to Titian's studio in Rome. Although Michelangelo had praised the style and colours of Titian's *Danaë*, he critically remarked what a mistake and a shame it was that Venetian painters were not taught to draw methodically from the very beginning of their career. Titian could be a great artist, if only he knew how to draw properly!

As in any anecdote, here too, behind personal criticism, there is a general judgement that one cannot be an excellent painter and artist without drawing skills and rigorous study. In reality, besides Titian, Vermeer and Velazquez, we could find many other examples where artists have achieved perfection in their painting without studying draftsmanship. Some historians even link the history of modern art with the decline of drawing, citing as evidence Manet, Cézanne, and even Picasso and Matisse, whose drawings apparently were not worth exhibiting.

Certainly, we could name many other famous figures from the past or present whom critics contend "cannot really draw". To this day, that remark remains a popular and indispensable part of the offensive

Petr Nikl, Hatching I, 1986

arsenal of those who want to attack a work of art they are reviewing one way or another. The Renaissance critical and artistic canon thus remains part of our postmodern reality, even though today's visual arts require radically different approaches and skills.

It is all the more interesting, then, that in this digitized, computerized, and generally technologized era, an artist should appear who is able to express himself in the current artistic language, yet still knows how to draw. This applies to Petr Nikl more than anyone else from the generation of Czech artists which appeared on the scene in the second half of the 1980s. Nikl is a great drawer, as documented both by his fantastical drawings and by his illustrations for his own books of stories, "mysteries", poetry or atlases of the most bizarre tools and creatures. At the same time, no one in today's Czech visual and theatre arts can rival not only the ideal of a technically efficient artist brimming with imagination, but also the more general ideal of the Renaissance man – inventor.

Nikl's original creative expression penetrates theatrical output and is also an essential part of the artist's poetic and linguistically sophisticated texts or musical works, leaving us at pains to find a comparison in this country. Nevertheless, in Nikl's work the Renaissance is not so much reflected in his creative range and overhang, as, much more, in the primitive attempt to *get to the bottom of things* and come up with something that has not been voiced, staged or depicted before. And so Petr Nikl, with the passion of Leonardo, has started assembling the most bizarre musical instruments, combining conceptual art with theatre and performance, or building a "Nest of Games" as an eminent area of the three foundational signs of human existence: imagination, playfulness and interactivity.

The imagination is boundless. This distinguishes it from knowledge, which is always limited. But what about a work of art where a seemingly broad consensus exists on knowledge of the meaning and significance thereof? Unlike the classic art of representation, modern art stands or falls on the process of interpretation and constant communication between the creator and those who are interested in his work as viewers, listeners or readers. That is why, as Umberto Eco says, openness defines a work of art.

Petr Nikl, Little Horses, 1991

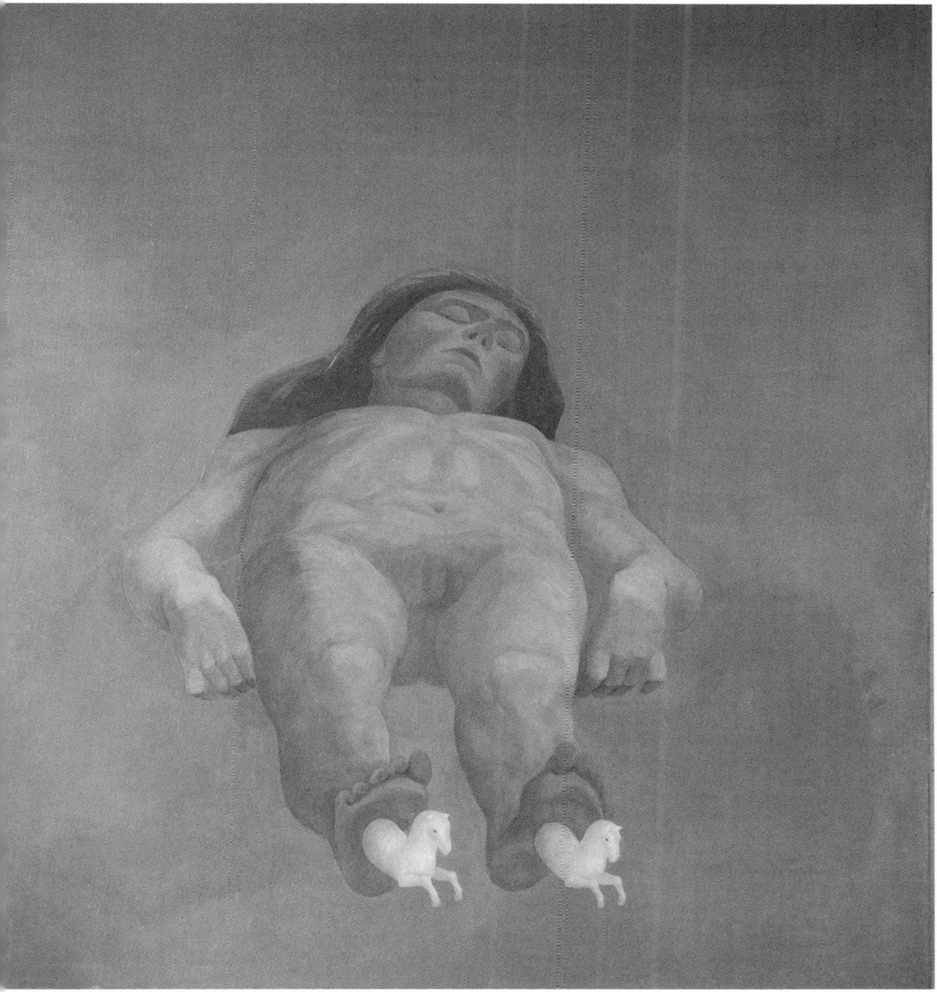

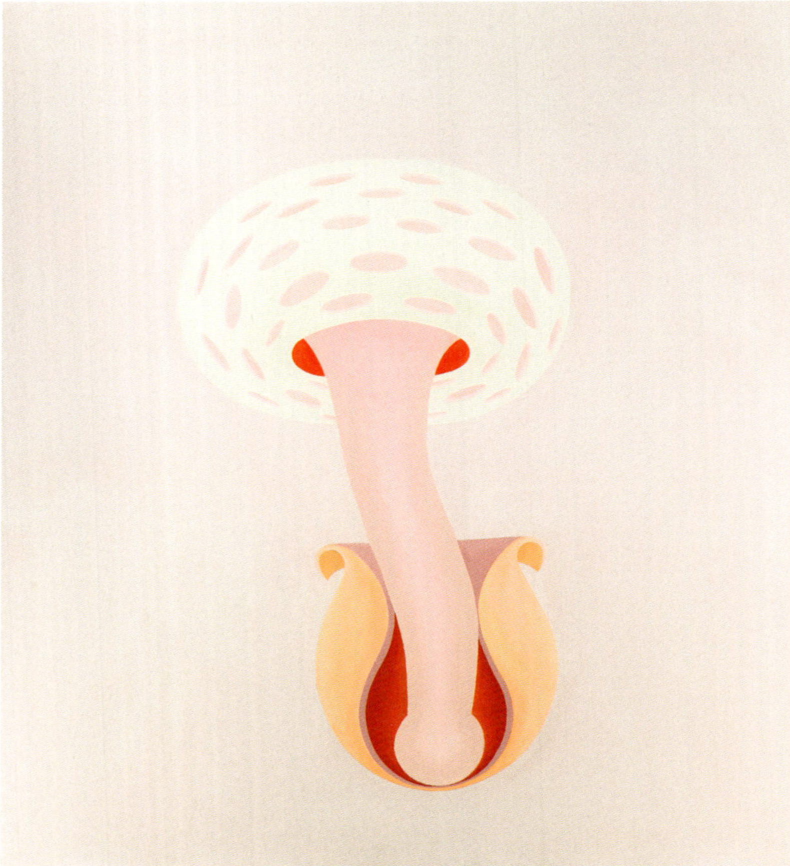

Much more than anywhere else, in art there are also clear rules of the *hermeneutic circle*, in which each meaning is both the result and starting point of the continuing process of interpretation. Each interpretation refers only to other meanings which someone else before us has already uncovered in another interpretive process. In the same way, our interpretations serve as the basis for future interpretive processes.

Petr Nikl, Russula, 2001

This basic hermeneutic experience means that, behind texts, we must look for other texts, as we are constantly reminded by Joyce's *Ulysses* and Coetzee's *Foe*. Behind images, we must search only for other images, as shown, for example, by Pablo Picasso in his masterful variations of Velázquez's famous picture of the noble girls of the Spanish royal court, *Las Meninas*. Velázquez's image is one of the most cited works of European painting; in it the painter, entirely freshly, addresses, for example, the issues of the interior and exterior of a depiction, or the intense relationship between the viewer and the event portrayed. As a result, we are now also able to grasp art as a particular expression of philosophical thinking. For instance, Foucault's fascination with Velázquez's picture in the book *The Order of Things* is eloquent proof of this.

In contrast, Picasso took formal features of the cited work and used them as signs and codes in his own paintings. Inspired by the

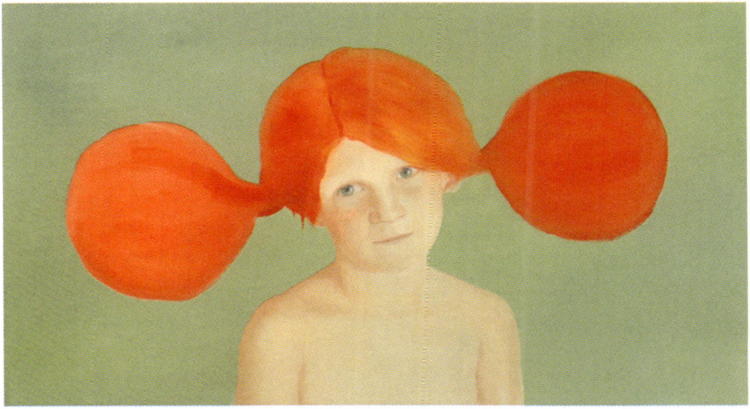

profundity of its model, Picasso's *Las Meninas* consistently guides us to other images, and not to a portrayal of any form of "natural world", whether the world of the royal court or anything else. Here, the artist, with his unique talent, foreshadowed our current situation, in which the philosophical and aesthetic possibility of describing "the world as it really is" has fallen apart. That is not to say that we live in

Petr Nikl, Anna as Pipi, 2004

an intellectually or culturally poorer or more parched world. On the contrary, we are faced with new ways of understanding ourselves and our inconsistent world.

A major feat in this sense is Nikl's series of monochrome canvases from the early 1990s. In these paintings, the artist generally borrows images from Italian Renaissance masters and moulds them with the power of his own imagination, transforming them so that ultimately no one can see the ideal Renaissance pitch, but breathtaking manifestations of Nikl's imagination, which are both admirable and disconcerting, and sometimes even frightening.

The force of perspective painting and original "tricks", with the shrinking of the feet and the shortening of the legs have been retained from Mantegna's image of the dead Christ, yet here, instead of a tortured male body, shrouded from the waist down, we are faced with an entirely uncovered young man who appears to be simply reposing on the canvas. In addition, from the feet, on which Mantegna originally realistically portrayed Christ's nail wounds, in Nikl's picture white horses are running out. Perhaps these are dreamt-of toys, perhaps just a playful dream?! Are these horses about to rush out of a dead body, or are they, in fact, part of the body, bearing it away through free space to an unknown place? And could they perhaps simply be more of those "dead toys", also installed by Nikl in the early 1990s?

Tangled and confused ideas about mythical centaurs mysteriously appear in a picture which Christians have associated with bare humanity and the infinite grace of God, death and salvation, for two thousand years. Other canvasses from the same series are dominated by images of boyish characters familiar from the Renaissance view of the Holy Family or the Virgin Mary with the Infant Jesus. The boys' hands, however, are either trapped in something resembling a beetle's body, or stuffed birds are hatching from the children's hands. And what are we to make of *Boy and Giraffe*, with the white stiff neck of a "giraffe" penetrating a baby's belly?

The psychoanalytic interpretation, with all references to the phallus and penetration, seems so obvious, it must be rejected as too superficial and reductive. Similarly, the *Flowers* series, containing canvases on which, for example, hyper-realistic paintings of orchids, with detailed elaboration, can easily be confused with the female genitals, ultimately undermines the credibility of any psychoanalysis, demonstrating, paradoxically, its validity and limitations. In this connection, during one of our conversations Petr Nikl protested: "But it really is an orchid!". Yes, even the psychoanalyst must acknowledge that there are situations and circumstances where *The Cigar is Just a Cigar*!

If the "*child* is the father of the man", as claimed by the psychologist Alfred Adler, then the child is also the father of Nikl's artefacts. However, this is no smiling, chubby little boy, over whose delightful speeches adults can gush and whose innocence and immediacy can be emotionally moving. Nikl's child is not morally uncorrupted and generally better than an adult, as Jean-Jacques Rousseau, in his time, dangerously and naively believed. Disturbing and traumatic images swim around in his mind that adults, in their "civilizedness", suppress and supplant. Yet this is precisely how the child knows better than an adult. His senses, imagination and fantasy are not yet encumbered with the weight of the everyday and the veil of social and intellectual convention.

Nikl's work, of course, has introspective features and the artist is constantly confronted with the lot of the "professional child" of a famous mother, whose original and sophisticated toys belong inherently to the childhood of all those who grew up in this country in the second half of the 20th century. Nikl has never denied his "excursions into childhood", which are also a "flight from everyday life" and a very intimate reconciliation with the premature death of his mother, and recently he quite systematically explored this important aspect of his work in the project *Dialogue with my Mother*.

Childhood is just as fascinating and idyllic as it is threatening and traumatic, but in particular it is a source of inherent wisdom and freedom. In this context, I can still see Nietzsche's famous phrase "In every real man a child is hidden that wants to play" printed on the cover of a selection of Morgenstern's poetry entitled *The Moonsheep*. Although the book was published as early as 1965, it was still cult grammar-school reading in the 1980s, alongside the work of Jacques Prévert and the bizarre novels of Boris Vian. Nor

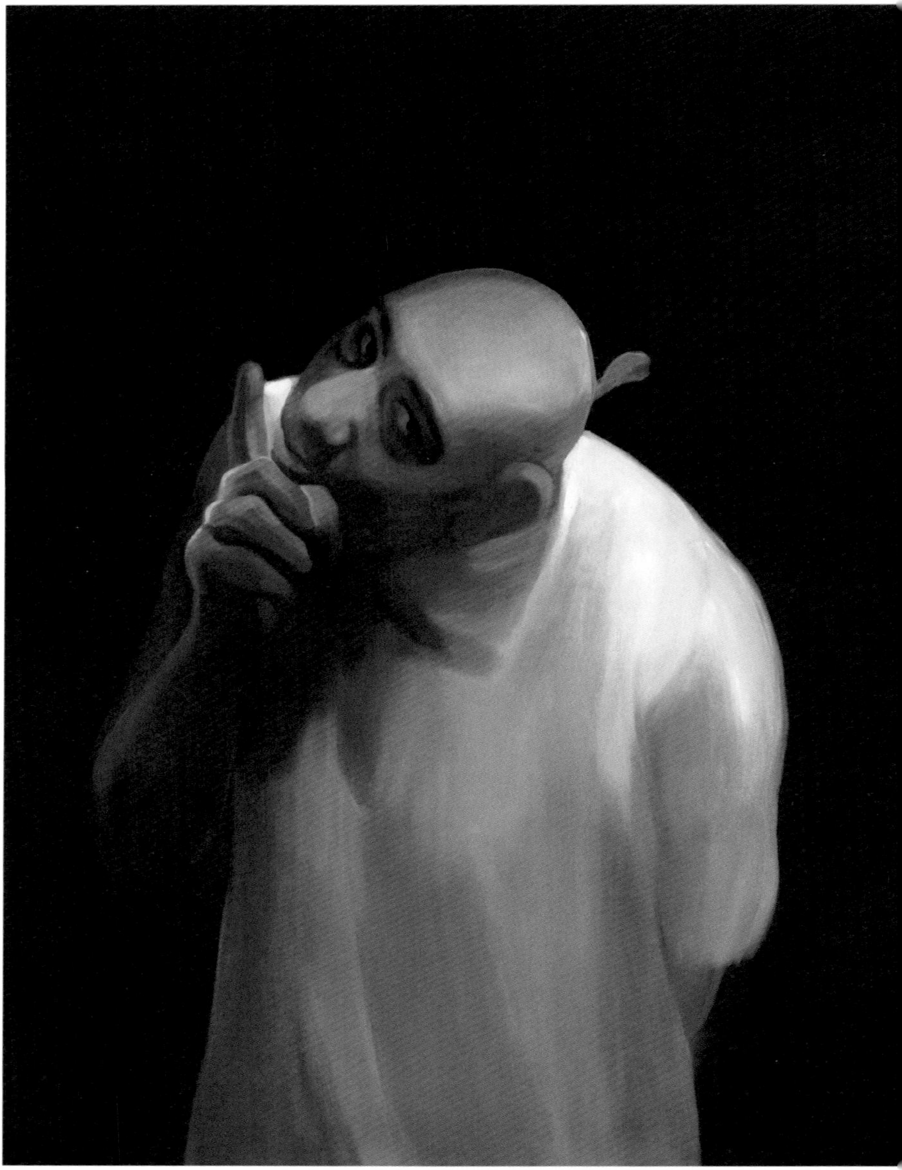

can we overlook how close the imagery and poetry of these authors is to Nikl's art.

Influenced by this literature, however, one realizes the fundamental difference between Nietzsche and Adler's "inner child". Unlike Adler's individually psychological point of view, Nietzsche, along with many other poets, writers and artists, relies on play as an alternative to all the world's seriousness, morality and philosophy. Spontaneity and play are a universal human need and a celebration of the irreverence and sprightliness particular to children and artists in a modern world obsessed with one's own seriousness and dignity. Indeed, Nietzsche notes that "We have art in order not to die of the truth". Albert Camus, in *The Myth of Sisyphus*, adds "To create is to live twice". While philosophical truth is just an example of the absurd world, artistic output is a way to maintain self-awareness and human dignity and uniqueness in such a world.

Nikl always focuses on grasping that common point where spontaneous energy and the natural human capacity for imagination develop as quickly as possible and in directions as diverse as possible. Since the late 1980s and the first series of imaginary animals and biomorphic compositions of cocoons, "hatchlings" and butterflies, Nikl's pictures have been funny and frightening, hopeful and sinister, prescient and mysterious. They are very poetic, but certainly have nothing to do with lyrical poetry. In this regard, they resemble the mythical and fairy tales which Nikl writes and transforms into music as much as he paints. Quite mysteriously in them, "golden snakes gold incense" so that "you cannot tell what is a snake and what is not", as in the song of the same title from Nikl's 2004 music album *Not Afraid of the Death's Head.*

The Dutch historian and anthropologist Johan Huizinga, in *Homo Ludens*, recognized that play was older than culture, and that every culture necessarily incorporates an element of play. Without play, that sovereign realm of freedom, in which no political, economic or other laws apply, no human community could exist, and everyone, sooner or later, would go mad in the face of tyranny of the serious world.

The artist is one of those who can stand up to such tyranny, and art in general is a feature of play, because it gives rise to completely new

Petr Nikl, Filip Pointing, 2004

imaginary worlds. This is also why, since ancient times, the mission of the artist has been linked with obsession and the exceptional gift of wisdom, which other mortals can only admire, unless, on the contrary, they feel outraged and incensed. Not surprisingly, there has always been a mutual jealousy, but also a deep reverence and respect, between charismatic artists on the one hand and philosophers or theologians on the other.

The Sisyphean fate of the modern man has been addressed not only by Albert Camus and other existentialists, but also, for example, by the German philosopher and phenomenologist Eugen Fink, according to whom what human wisdom does is rather like a Sisyphean task. It is worth noting that Fink says this in his *Play as Symbol of the World*, at the end of which he arrives at the paradoxical notion of the world as "playerless play" which ultimately best represents its super-human nature. Such a world can be understood only through symbols, although these obviously fail to capture its overall importance and are always only of a fragmentary nature.

In this light, since the Renaissance, humankind has tried all the more to improve reality through art. Even Nikl's paintings of flowers, plants or fungi, in which the wild visuality of original natural shapes and open sexual imagery and symbolism compete side by side, are one such attempt to improve reality. Similarly, in reality it would be most unlikely for us to encounter the faces from Nikl's series of the same name. Such an original simply has to be painted.

The common denominator of Nikl's images, texts, songs or performances is therefore certainly no version of a Schopenhauerian "world as will and representation", but rather a notion of the world as endless play, and the movement of signs and meanings and the sharing thereof with the broadest possible surroundings. Nikl allows himself to be guided by Nietzsche's "inner child", which would much rather tap into Dionysian dithyrambs and share them as intensely as possible with viewers and listeners than listen, with good manners, to the tones of flutes played by shepherds from idyllic Arcadia. Boldly and freely, he constantly re-embarks on a dangerous game with human imagination and tries to communicate, through various symbolic expressions, the non-communicable, namely the power and the boundaries of humanity itself in such "a world in play".

THE ART OF RECYCLING

THE “UNCULTIVATED” VISUAL LAYERING IN THE WORK OF PETR PÍSAŘÍK

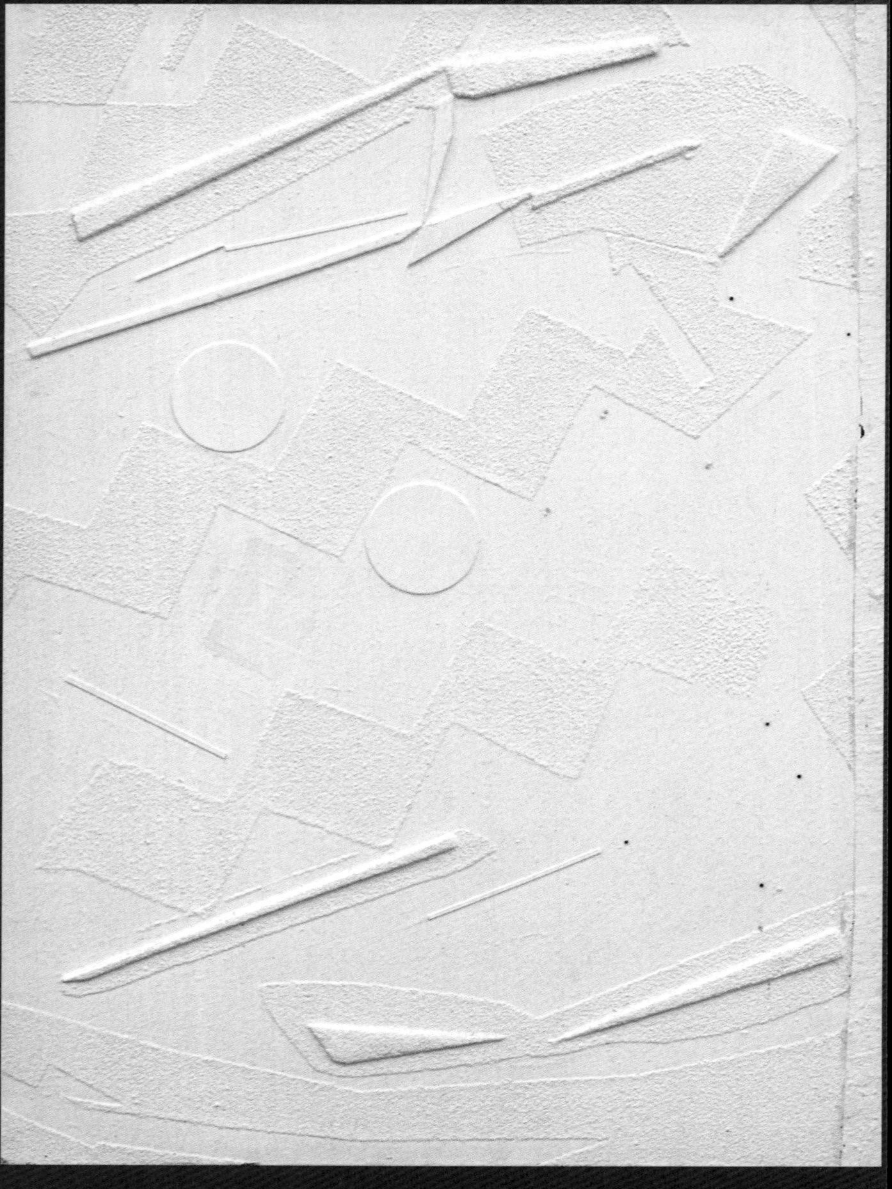

The Art of Recycling

The "Uncultivated" Visual Layering in the Work of Petr Písařík

One of the most powerful experiences during my stay in South Africa was a visit to a village inhabited by members of the Ndebele people. A university colleague promised me a trip to places off the beaten tourist track near Pretoria, so we made our way among local farms and ended up in an Ndebele village, the sleepiness of which was no different from a Sunday afternoon in a Czech village. While the local boys played football, their fathers looking on drinking beer, and the women in the crowd alternately chanted and talked while creating both traditional beaded artefacts and purely tourist souvenirs with incredible skill. Their singing was mirrored in their strictly geometrically decorated bead skirts, bracelets and necklaces perhaps more clearly than the sound of music in paintings by František Kupka. Even Piet Mondrian would have envied these women their feeling for colourful compositions of blue, yellow and red beads.

All the greater was my surprise when I discovered that the models for this abstract imagination were purely modern utility items, such as razors, introduced to the Ndebele by European colonists and traders. Also, the vast majority of beads used in South Africa since the 19th century have traditionally come from Europe, and even from Bohemia, so Jablonec jewellery has played an important role in this form of intercultural communication.

This very special and extraordinary clash of modern culture and traditional art is still evolving and constantly developing. Thanks to the superior beading skills of the Ndebele women, surpassing those of all other African nations, artefacts are being produced today that are visually inspired by the geometric morphology of purely contemporary technological creations, such as pylons or bulbs.

Compared with the works of their grandmothers, which were "minimalist" in colour, today's Ndebele women have fallen under the

Petr Písařík, Untitled, 2010

spell of colour "expression". The decorations of the village houses are also full of colours and, for me, all this blending of tradition and modernity was crowned by the sight, in the middle of a Kupka-esque traditional "razor" composition, of the unmistakable logo of the BMW circle split into four symmetrically alternating blue and white areas. At this point, all the painstakingly constructed knowledge and the dichotomy of pure and applied arts, tradition and modernity, as well as industry and crafts and the natural and technical world, disintegrated in my mind. In the setting African sun, it was as if all of us standing in the middle of the village at that moment had suddenly returned to the bosom of our anthropologically shared Eve, mother of all the living, who embarked on an uncertain, tentative journey across the world from here millions of years ago.

A year later, when I had the opportunity to see Chris Ofili's denigrated canvases in London, in contrast to the silly tabloid reports offended by the artist's use of elephant dung in his works, I was in awe of the reverence and sensitivity with which Ofili worked with the beads, those connecting lines between European and African cultures, tradition and modernity. It was as if Ofili wanted to say, through all this, that we do not only share an inexhaustible human imagination, but also the diverse tools and materials which we use to express it and which can travel in time and space, i.e. both in human history and from one continent to another.

In contemporary art, the boundlessness of which was meant to be captured, in its time, by the term postmodernism, the most admirable trait is the ability to travel and move in time and space without the worry that the artist in question will be accused of eclecticism, unoriginality or even plagiarism and general degeneration.

If today's Czech art scene has an artist capable of moving with the same ease as, for example, Chris Ofili, then that person is Petr Písařík. I do not intend this to be a superficial comparison of approaches to similar materials, whether decorative beads or gaudy colours. Nor am I interested in such significant differences, for instance, in approaches to the problem of cultural and personal identity, which is one of the central themes of Ofili's work but of marginal relevance to Písařík. I am more

Petr Písařík, Cuba libre, 2007

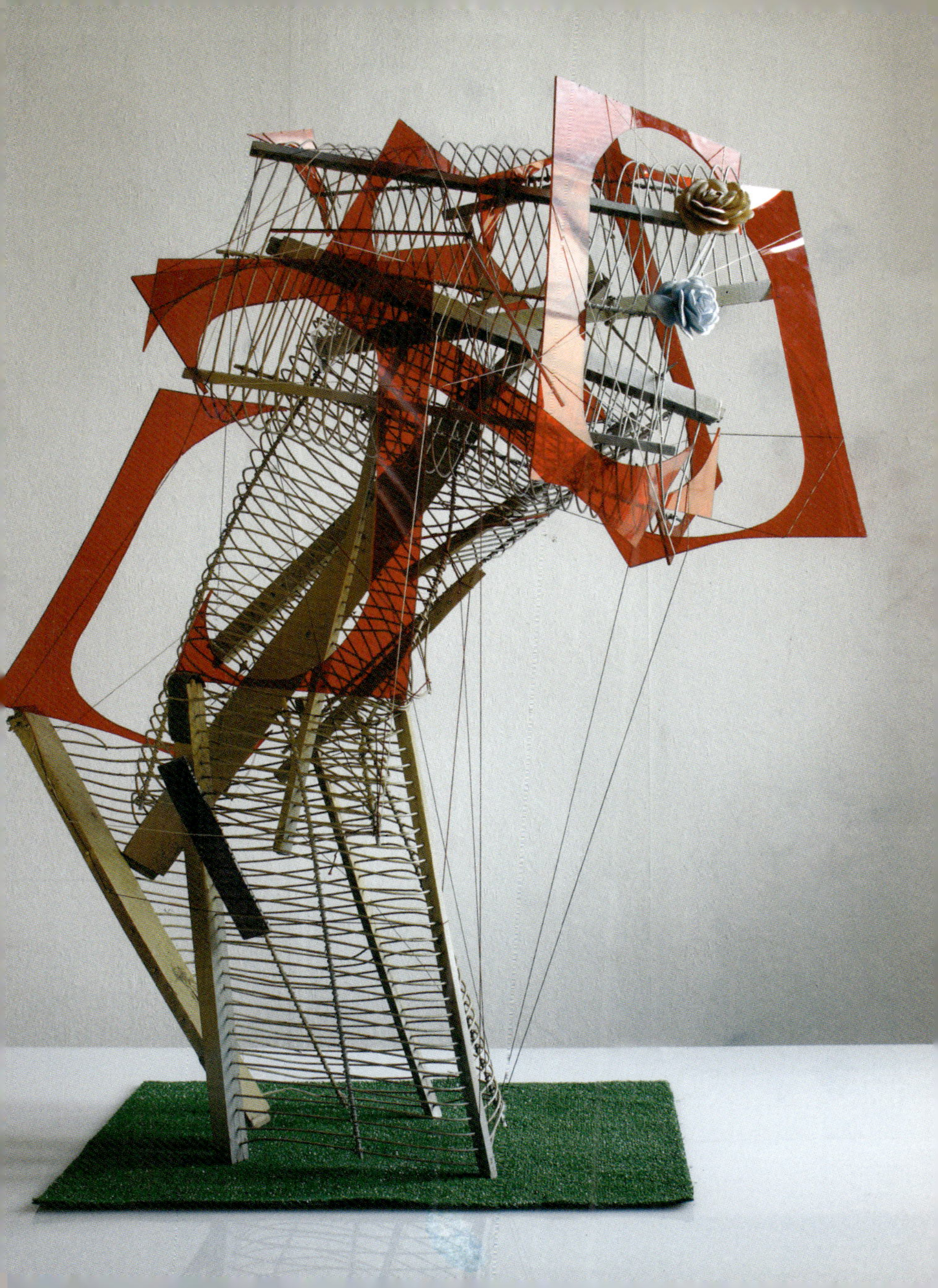

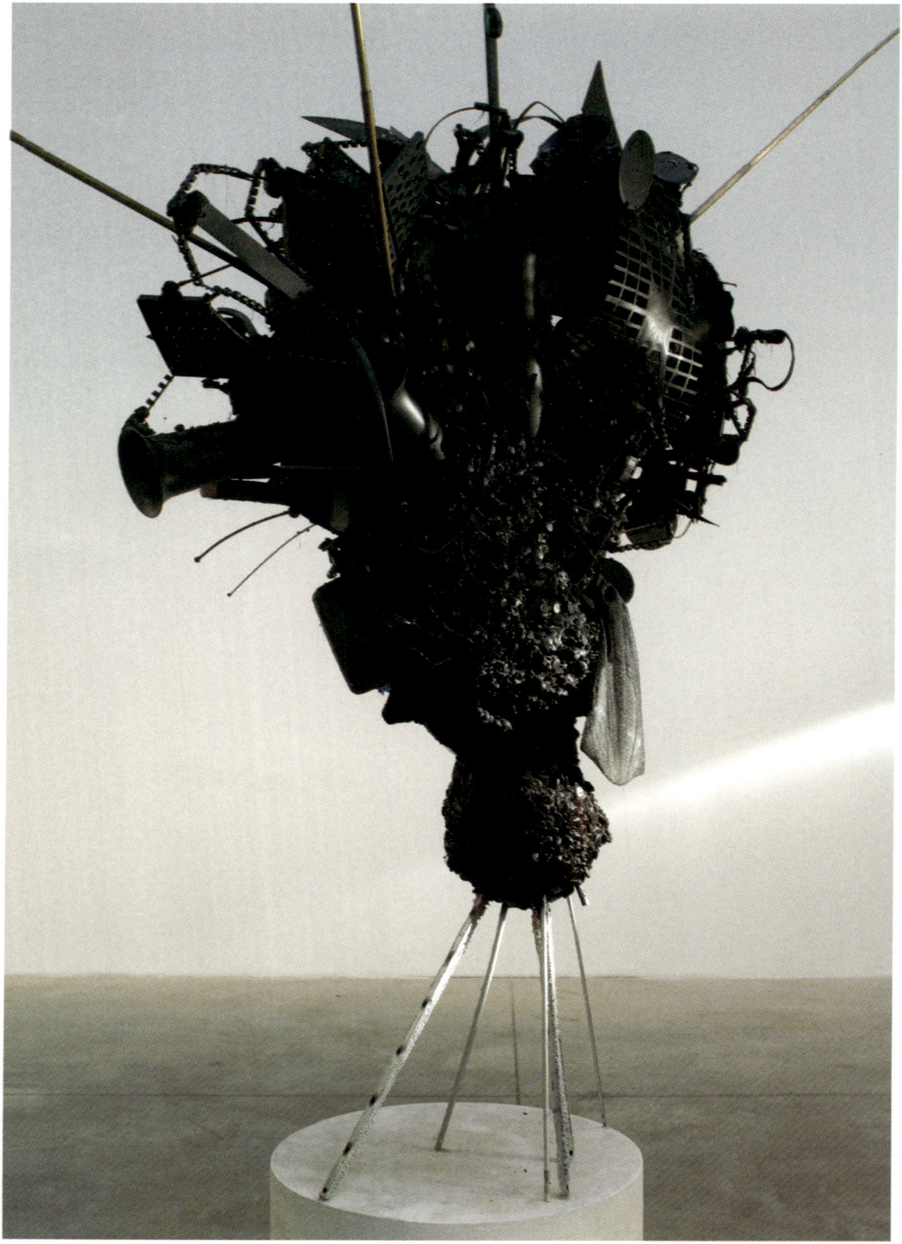

engrossed by the journeys of human imagination, which can combine infamous visual clichés with numbing and breathtaking beauty, and decorative restlessness with strict composition. Like Ofili, Písařík is an artist who can combine the most diverse art forms and manifestations in showy superficiality and thus refute the widespread objection of anti-aestheticism that art should not be decorative or, in particular, too "nice". In such work, on the contrary, decoration plays a key role, whether it involves beads, signal colours and samplers, ornately arranged clippings from pornographic magazines, floral embroidery, poppy grains, elephant dung or industrial waste.

Modernity is generally a state of tension between reality and potentiality. Reality is insufficient, with a plethora of ways to change and transform it into a new reality. In contrast to the given conditions of the world, plans have been elaborated in detail and rationally designed on how to change the world and re-narrate its "realistic" self-perceptions. Modernism has always been part of such narratives and viewed itself as an opportunity to stand out from the tight framework of reality and existing forms of life. Thus, at approximately the same time that Wassily Kandinsky was gradually removing all traces of the natural world from his paintings to achieve object-less abstract art, Arnold Schoenberg was delivering atonal music and James Joyce, in Ulysses, was breaking established ideas about what the European novel should look like.

Yet the abandonment of objectivity in the visual arts, the condemnation of classical tonality and the demolition of the novel composition did not mean surrendering to the power of rational calculus, but rather anticipated the intensification of the inner artistic experience. This is why, for example, Mondrian's abstract compositions or Klee's new mythology of nature are incomprehensible without the surreal avant-garde. In other words, where Kandinsky used a sharp brush stroke, Dalí and Buñuel, in the film with *An Andalusian Dog*, directly used a razor to cut into eyes, so that these eyes could see the world subject to the logic of the dream.

Postmodernism, in contrast, is modernism bereft of internal tension, aware of the quicksand of the ideas and imperatives on which its own

Petr Písařík, Martian Revivalist, 2007–2008

foundations are built. No "new beginning" is convincing enough and no "new foundation" is firm enough to warrant the all-out demolition of reality and the building of a "new world". Reality suddenly shows itself to be fuller than the possibilities of replacing it, and the human imagination must, surprisingly, come to terms much more with a technically ever more quickly changing world. Whereas, in the modernist period, reality never lived up to its potential, in the postmodern age, potential itself became the defining sign of reality.

However, such a postmodern dictate of the present carries the significant risk that we will stop understanding the past, that we will lose accountability in relation to the future, and that we will consider everything contemporary, without further distinction, to be important. Nevertheless, there is a possible way out of this risk: to return, reflexively, to modern artistic and cultural forms, to impress on them another expression, and, without avant-garde gestures, to reflect on their possible links with purely utility articles, amateurly kitsch decorations and other cultural artefacts. It is possible only in such deep reflection, in today's visually and otherwise overloaded era, to create an original art form and language.

This is how Petr Písařík sees his work; he is loosely inspired by modernist abstraction or constructivism and traditional landscapes and still lifes, a genre loved by all amateur "Sunday" painters. In Písařík's works, industrial design and artificial materials are naturally combined with the visions of abstract art that Cubists, Orphists and other great experimenters of the early decades of the last century used to have. The decorative fabric patterns and utility items from the later 1960s, when seductive forms of consumerism began, after a delay, to penetrate even Czech society, are again very close to the Russian pre-war avant-garde.

Decorative objects carved out of roots and branches and other kitsch typical for high-rise flats are used by the artist without parody or ironic aloofness, as required by the canon of "serious art", because even this "bad art" conceals human creativity, playfulness and a desire for self-expression and the beautification of one's surroundings, i.e. given anthropological conditions that precede any art. Even Petr Písařík's exhibitions are original works of art as they always function as original installations focusing just as much on specific images or objects as on the overall structure and composition.

According to the modern idea, the aesthetic standards of high art are gradually penetrating lower areas of culture and replacing the old standards. Sometimes this takes the form of a sudden break, and other times it is gradual, spread over very long time periods. The high may be inspired by the low and continue alongside it, but eventually its layer will predominate and penetrate the whole of culture. In contrast, postmodernism has abandoned these claims of higher versus lower and the notion of the one-way influence of the aesthetic standards of high art on general culture. The picture, both literally and figuratively speaking, is becoming a surface filled with multiple meanings and cultural influences following multiple paths.

Písařík's images and objects are full of artistic and cultural forms that have already had some meaning or other, whether a means of expression of avant-garde modernism, industrial decor from old drapery, souvenirs, plastic articles, commercial packaging and DIY products. The citation of Mondrian's geometric purism here goes hand in hand with the industrial use of colours and sequins found on the clothes of the women of Karlín and on the modelled nails of their daughters.

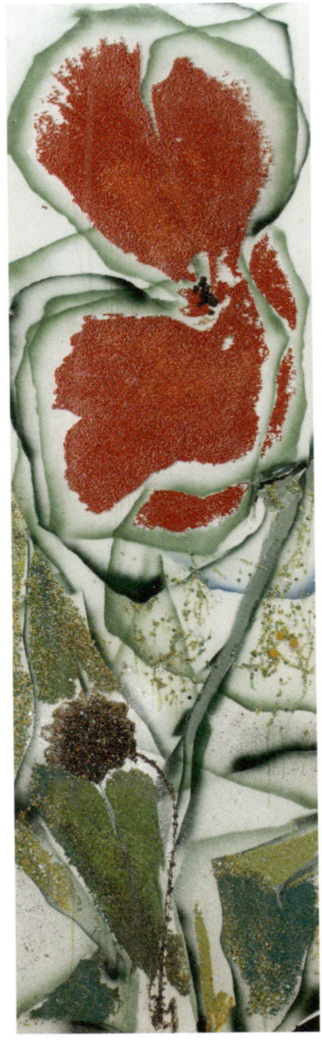

Petr Písařík, While I Was Tying a Bouquet, 2007–2008

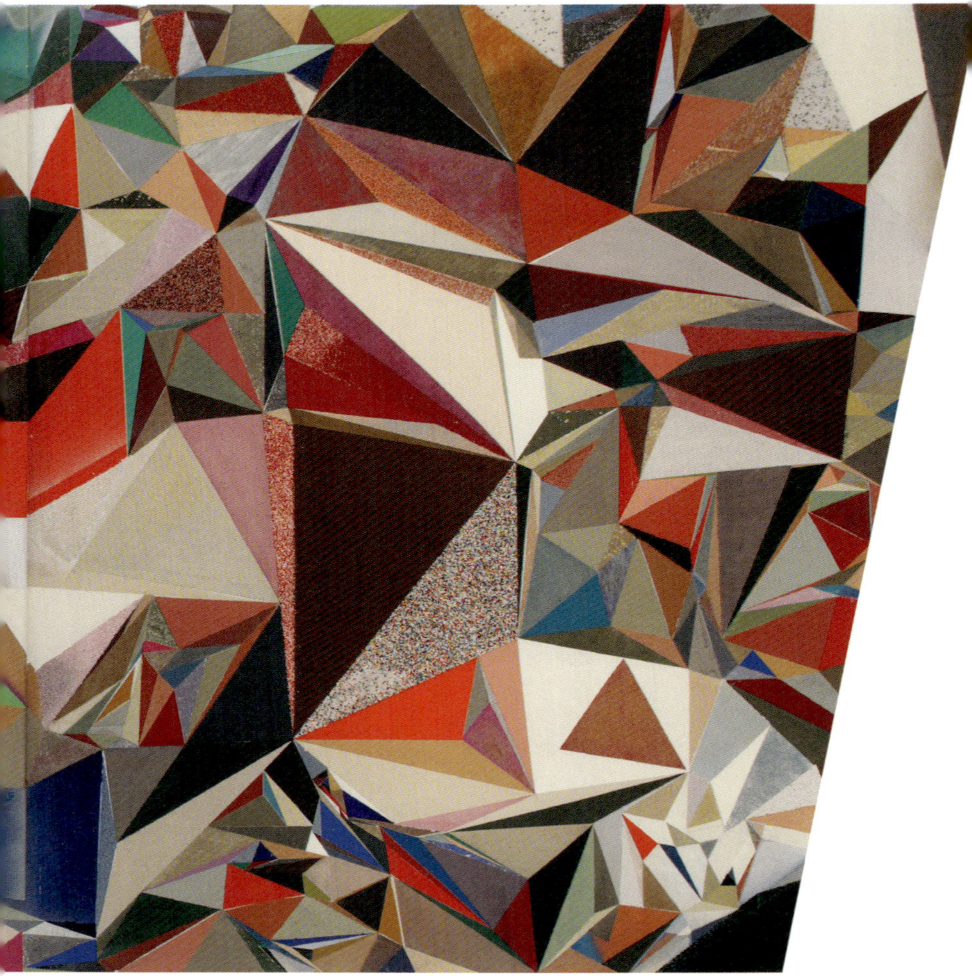

Písařík's artistic method consists of the dissolution of the linear narrative of art, the recycling, overlaying and interspersing of various art forms, and the suspense created by the choice of different artistic means. This combination eloquently shows that the differentiation between artistic artefacts and everyday objects of our consumerist culture has much more porous borders than we are usually willing to admit. Everyone knows that original artistic vision is always reflected in modern design. Few would realize, however, that it is also possible to cut or tear up and re-assemble ordinary water pipe insulation to look like houseplants in the context of art. What is more, Písařík uses, for instance, the purple spray paint popular among graffiti artists in their concrete jungles in order to encumber these "flowers", made up of building materials, even more from a civilizational aspect, and thus enhance their disturbingly melancholic aura.

The artistic image is not clear, but ambiguous. It is neither a mathematical formula, nor a mere pictogram, but always concentrates multiple meanings, even though, for example, the theme is predetermined and straightforward. While playing with ambiguity is indeed an attribute of postmodernism, Písařík takes it further, into play with a multiplicity of visual forms, where the difference between high and low no longer applies and where the logical design of the interior art form is as important as completely spontaneous creative expression in the style of outsider art. The geometric form here has the same importance as the mass of colour that spills under the template. The wildest, seemingly endless decoration is as important as the painter's collected, concentrated expression. The fragile vulnerability of poppies, for example, gives way to the power of loud colours that would be difficult to find even among bouquets of crepe roses offered in the shooting gallery of any village fair. Spray paint and gaudy sequins, for their part, create compositions on plywood surfaces that you would seek in vain even in the made-in-China "electric pictures" sold at Czech markets.

The power of the "cheap" image here surpasses any notional effect of the "most expensive" plasma screen. It offers us eye candy in its original form, which does not yet distinguish between the lowliness of kitsch and the heights of art. Písařík achieves the same power by

Petr Písařík, Super Position, 2008

apparently just sprinkling poppy seeds into a combination of acrylic and industrial enamel paints, ultimately turning this abstract composition into *Malevich's Wallpapers*, the radicalism of which might even give this maestro of modernism cause to learn from Písařík.

Modernism has always been expressed by extreme means, but Malevich's *White on White* is a boundary that cannot be beaten by anything more extreme. However, the limitation of Malevich's famous work can be easily surpassed by exploiting the extreme nature of white paint and incorporating further shapes or objects onto the blank surface, the shading of which will change depending on the variability of daylight and artificial lighting. Rhomboids or flowers rising to the surface of Písařík's canvas thus open up dramatic shadow play. Yet this is not entirely controlled by either the artist or the person installing the picture in a particular place, because the shadow play is also affected by the variability of daylight determined by the astronomical laws of the Earth's rotation around the Sun.

Despite the traditional form of his paintings and objects, in some respects Písařík's output resembles work with a computer, on which you can run several applications at once and seek mutual links between them, as well as the overall sense opening up at the interface of those individual applications. The transitions are more important than the limits.

In the 1990s, in Western Europe and the US, postmodernism occasionally became synonymous with a lifestyle and culture in which the pace is dictated by a lack of restriction, monetary ideas, wit, and the motto "Anything's goes". In this respect, Písařík's art, although full of wit, is not subject to the postmodern terror of topicality and immediate commentary. Písařík's images and objects are typified by lightness, but by no means frivolity or mere fun. Though not tenacious, they try to find meaning in play and in the concurrence of various cultural and artistic levels and layers. It is the playful capacity for such layering that gives rise to their artistic originality and the cultural overlap of their uniqueness, comparable perhaps only to the creations of women from the African Ndebele people.

DIALOGUE WITH THE INNER VOICE OF THE ARTIST AND THE IMAGE

WHAT IS "BEYOND" JAN MERTA'S PAINTINGS

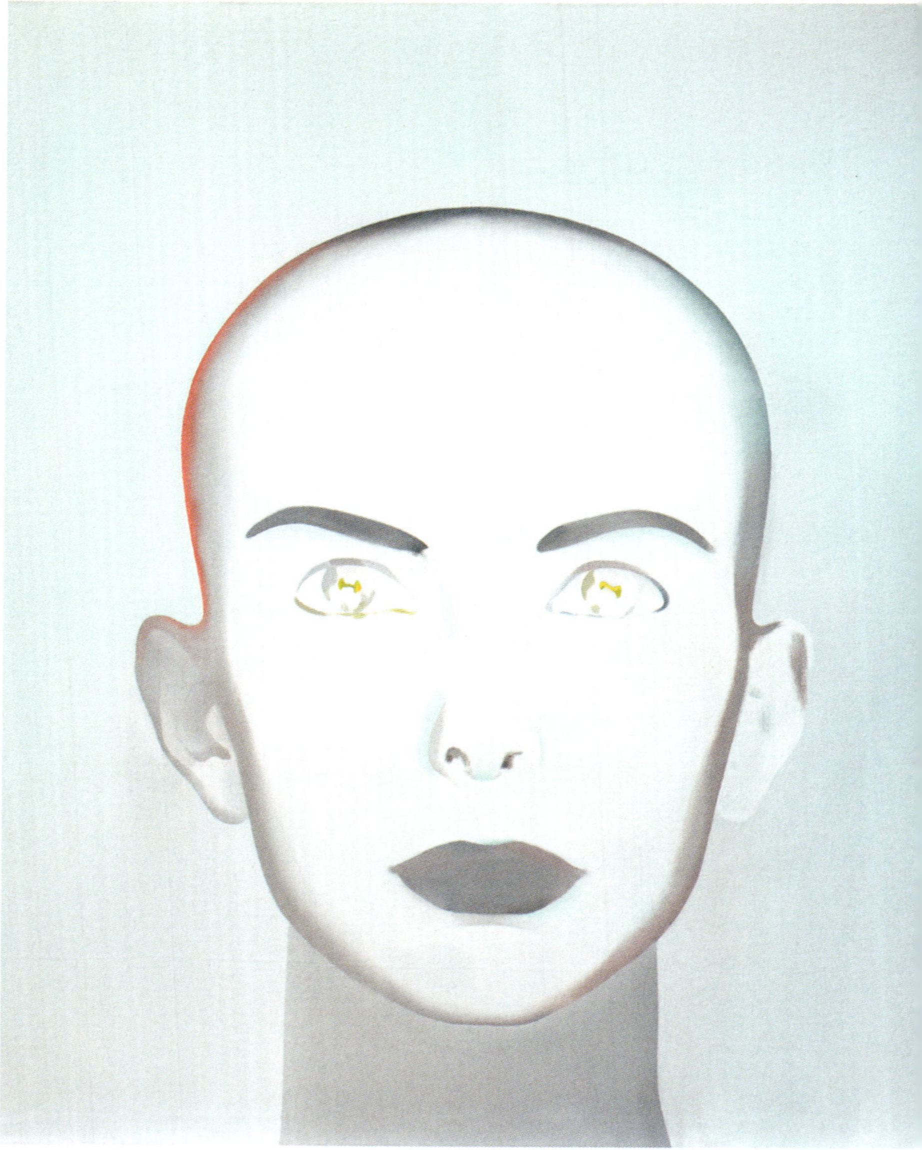

Dialogue with the Inner Voice of the Artist and the Image

What is "Beyond" Jan Merta's Paintings

There is almost nothing harder than writing about the paintings of Jan Merta. Of course, one could expand on how they are both poetic and analytical, concrete and abstract, or concentratedly serious yet frivolously ironic. All this is true, but also depressingly banal, and only hinders the discussion about what is at the core of Merta's art and what is concealed behind each painting. The essence of Merta's concentrated and artistically rich and refined expression is the ability of unifying transcendence, which can hardly be captured in words, without the viewer either excessively speculating about a work or missing it entirely.

For these reasons, I remained reluctant to write about the work of Jan Merta for a long time, although I had always considered it one of the highlights of Czech postmodern art. Moreover, when, at the Zdeněk Sklenář Gallery in spring 2010, the artist exhibited his *Stockhausen Symphony*, a series of paintings in which, with a clear moral gesture, he caricatured a portrait of the composer who called the attack on the World Trade Centre in New York on 11 September 2001 "the greatest work of art that is possible in the whole cosmos", I came to the conclusion that writing about Merta's work is impossible because every word is unnecessary even before it is written. In *Karlheinz Stockhausen Performs his Zyklon B Symphony*, the artist, in supremely visual (although for many of his admirers certainly controversial) language, spells out quite directly what the boundaries of art are and where the artist's freedom of expression ends and where the path is opened to murder and total destruction, the political and aesthetic celebration of which was honed by Nazism to perverse perfection.

Therefore, when it came to Merta's work, I decided to abide by Wittgenstein's view that one must remain silent about that which one

Jan Merta, Ideal Radiant III, 2000

is unable to speak. Yet the impossible will not let us rest, and so we constantly return to it and examine the conditions and circumstances under which such impossibility eventually becomes possible. Over time, I realized that the cause of my reluctance to speak and write about Merta's paintings was actually the fear that I would butt into the transcending inner voice that the artist lets speak from his images. The only way to break the silence while not interrupting Merta's artistic speech could be to establish a dialogue with that voice.

Conversation between an artist and his own work is a creative method by means of which Karel Čapek made a unique contribution to the history of the European modernist novel. When his novel *War with the Newts* results in apocalyptic carnage between the victorious legions of newts and modern humankind, Čapek's narrator decides to stop the story and start conversing with himself about how the whole disaster could and should end. At this stage, the newt colonies are already occupying Dresden, having successfully invaded Russia, and the first newts have appeared in the Vltava river in Prague. The author certainly avoids alleviating the task with some divine intervention *ex machina* to draw the novel, after the model of classical tragedy, to a clear denouement and conclusion. Rather, he ponders everything in depth and arrives at the discouraging conclusion that the greatest threat to modern civilization is not unlikely lizards, cosmic catastrophe or divinely-delivered apocalypse, but humanity itself.

Instead of a final apocalypse, he offers a gloomy story about how the originally unified newt species may, over time, be divided into nations which start to kill each other off until complete self-destruction. People will then descend from the remaining islands to the coast again and will start to talk about the flood sent down by God on humanity for its sins, and about legendary countries such as England or France, which were supposedly the cradle of human culture. When the author's *inner* voice asks what happens then, he answers frankly: "I don't know what happens next."

In his famous novel *Krakatit*, a "fairy-tale grandfather" converses with the totally exhausted, fleeing Prokop when he is in a daze. The grandfather does not give a reply to Prokop's question about whether

Jan Merta, To the Welders (Farewell, Maestro), 2000

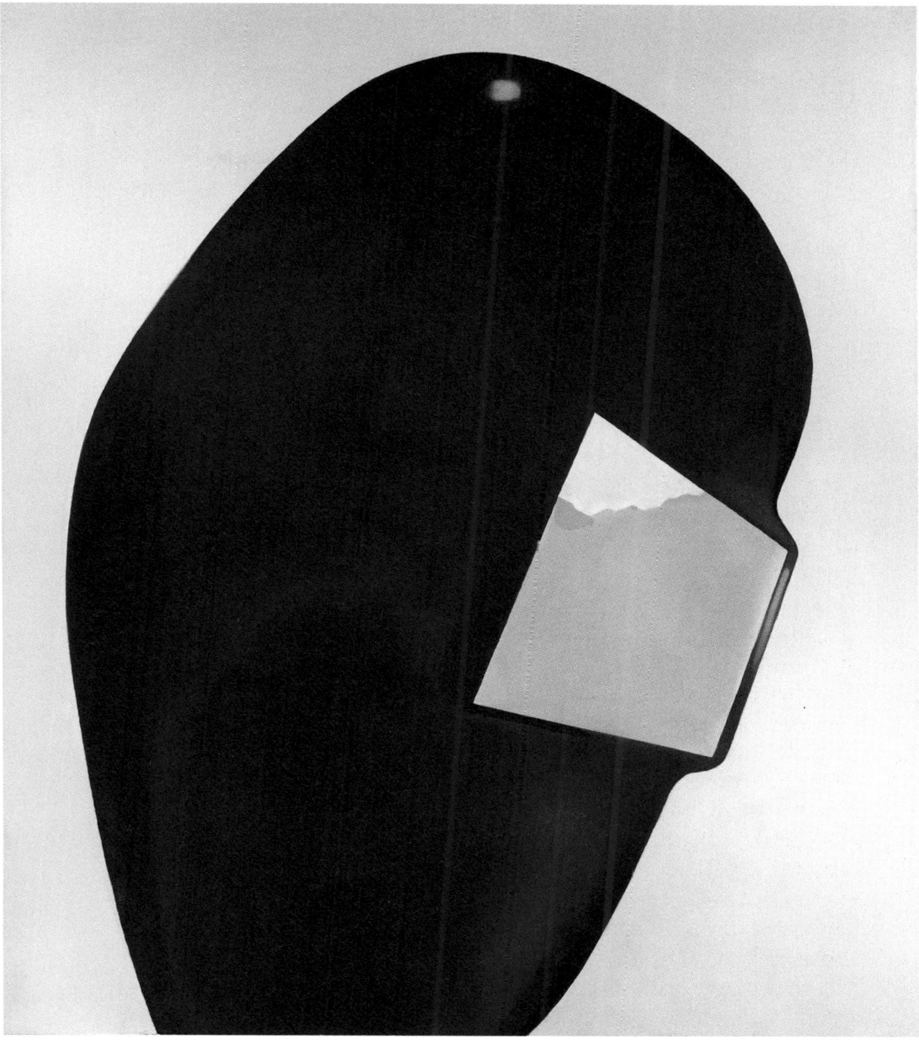

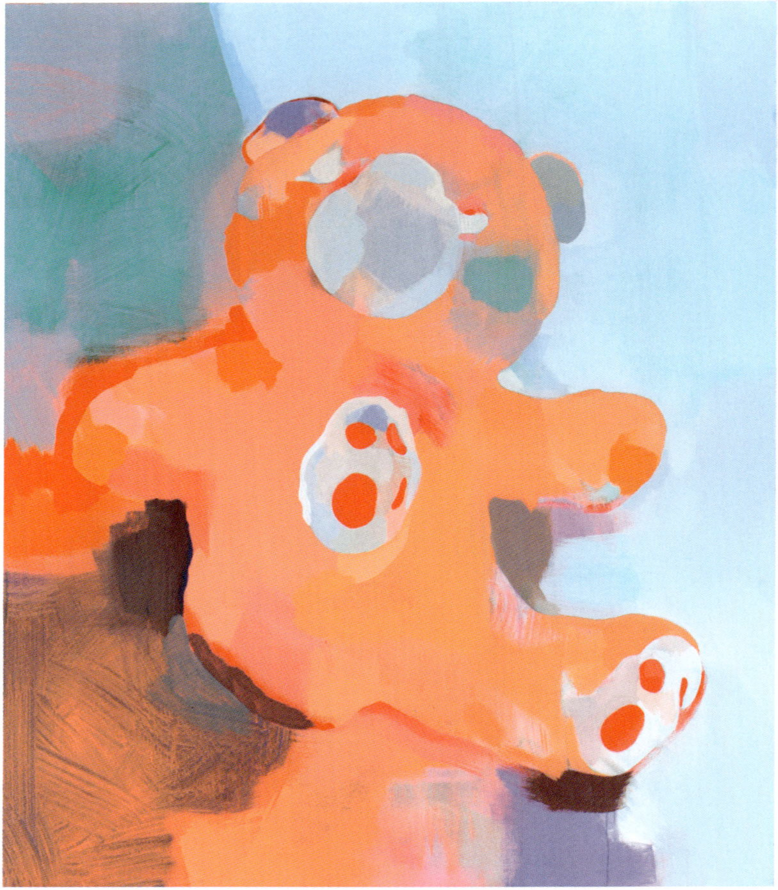

he had been bad, but instead notes that one "should think more than feel." If we forcefully hurtle into everything up to our ears and want the absolute, its power will eventually destroy us and tear us apart.

Jan Merta, Partner (from the triptych Meggi and Partner), 1999–2006

Therefore, rather than saving or breaking the world, humankind should focus instead on remaining whole and identifying and researching what is good and useful for people.

In no other art work of the present time is the artist's inner voice as clearly audible as in the paintings of Jan Merta. As in Čapek's experiments with the novel and literary structures, it is evident how the artist struggles with himself and explores the form and possible meanings of his own work, instead of relying on an artistic deity that would ex machina provide his paintings with a predetermined meaning and simple denouement.

Much like Karel Čapek did with literature in his time, Jan Merta likes to experiment in his paintings and choose different means of expression, including purely postmodern quotes and fragments, open metaphors and symbols, and depictions of faces which mirror not the human being, but the entire universe. Merta's canvases thus resemble stories or narratives in which the reader must immerse himself, requiring more thought than feeling, just as the fairy-tale grandfather advises Prokop in *Krakatit*. The inner voice also prevents us, for example, from making an aesthetic canon out of total destruction, as the Nazis did in an extreme form, but as our modern culture has had it inherently encoded at least since Romanticism.

The final form of such an internal dialogue by the artist with himself is then, quite naturally, the result of continuous exploration and the search for connections and possibilities of expression and the different meanings that can be revealed in a composition. In this respect, Merta's images are smart and knowledgeable without being ornate. They are intellectually provocative without succumbing to snobbish mannerisms. Their diversity is ultimately dominated by the recollection and unity of the inner voice, used by the artist to communicate not only with his audience, but also with what he has before him: with the work itself.

The process of creation is then a constant effort to liberate artistic expression from all external randomness, and to capture in an individual expression that which carries a general and timeless statement. And an important shift occurs round about here, because, unlike Čapek's novels, it is not just the artist, but also the image itself, which speaks with an

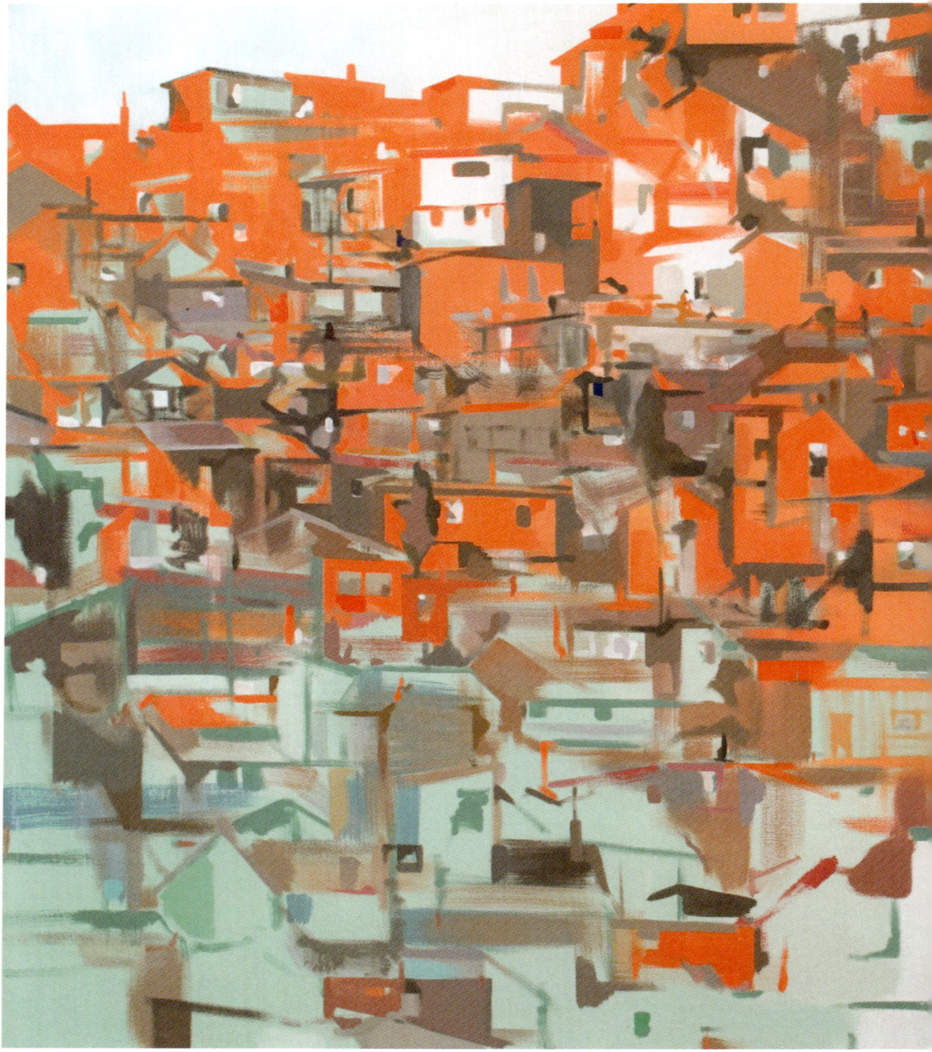

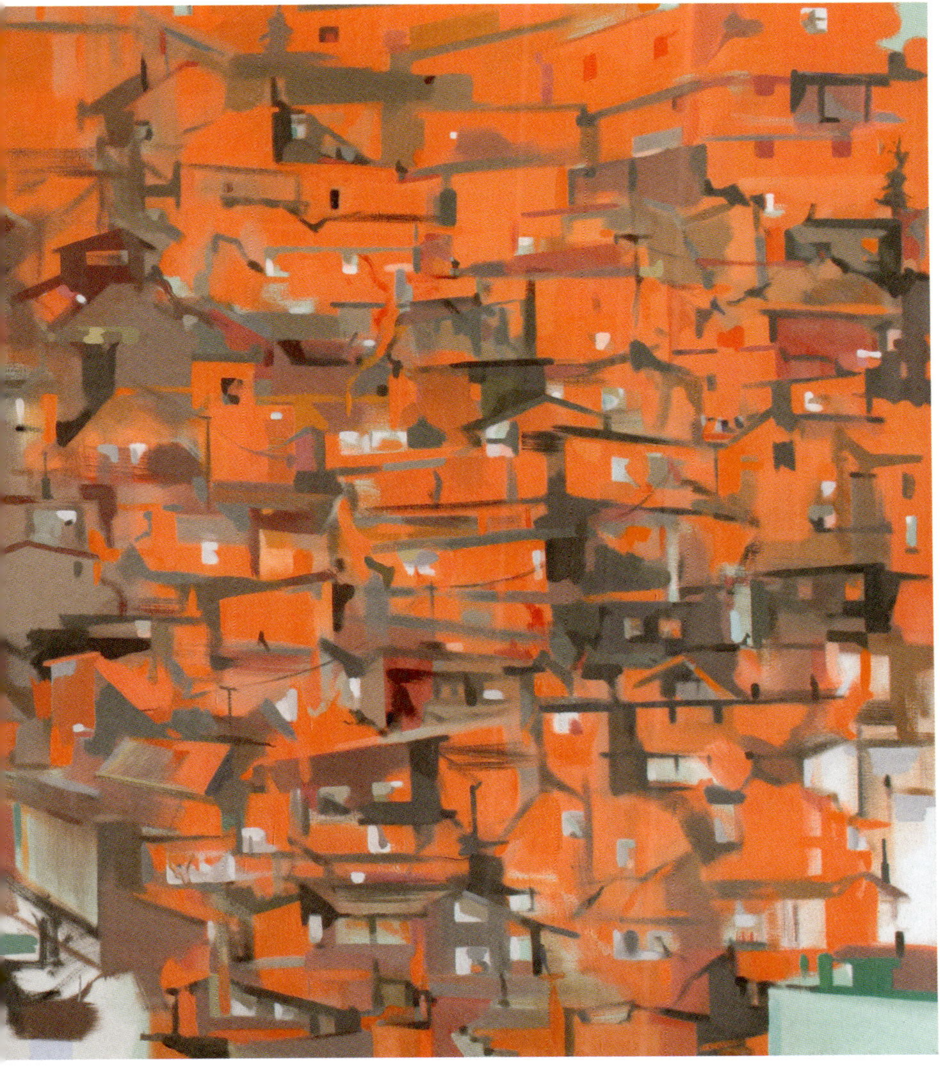

Jan Merta, Red Slum, 2002–2006

inner voice in Merta's paintings. It is precisely in the spirit of postmodern aesthetics that Merta's work converses with itself, which means that the viewer must listen to it with extreme concentration and attention.

Merta's pictures have their own language which is sometimes factual, other times metaphorical, and can be clear and bright as much as ambiguous and blurred. Nevertheless, the inner voice of Merta's images is comprehensive; in my personal opinion, his most important features are his vertical lines and the ability to compose a whole from fragments, and, conversely, to conceive of the whole only as a meaning-making fragment.

In the grey monochrome Vista from 1993, a rock rises into the sky that is stupefying in its prehistoric natural monumentality, but humankind has attached railings around its summit, so that, with a little imagination, the viewer could just as well see in his mind's eye the monumental steel bow of an ocean liner. The specific image depicted is not as important as the actual concept of the vista, from which we can see the world from a different, higher perspective. The famous *Big Shopping* from the same period shows a cluster of hanging plastic bags, which could just as easily be wings, over which a sky-blue wedge opens in grey space. Eyes stare upwards not only in several images of pollen clouds, but also in the dramatic composition *Cabin* (1995–1997), where something that has only the most general features of human habitation, i.e. an enclosed space and a window to look out of, is attached to a green mountain massif. Conversely, in another of Merta's pictures, a Sputnik hurtles to the ground, as indeed have so many other human inventions since the time of the myth of Icarus.

Similarly abstracted features and a sharply vertical composition can also be found in the eloquently entitled *A Funicular Is Leaving a Silent Worker* (1992–1997), where, in the free grey space between the clouds, an orange body remotely resembling this means of transport passes through. The most dramatic of all is certainly *Mountain Morsel* (1992–1997), where something vague balances on a mountain ridge which resembles an overhanging rock, but unsettles the viewer because it is uncertain and unsaid, and this contrasts sharply with the clear situation that dominates the overall composition.

Verticality can be found not only in the images of rock faces, clouds, the sky or the work entitled *The Pale Heart Stood Long above the Horizon* (1977–1995), but also in one of Merta's most spiritual canvases, *They Lived to See the Rising* (1999–2000), the name and overall mood of which appears to refer to the Gospel story of the women who were first

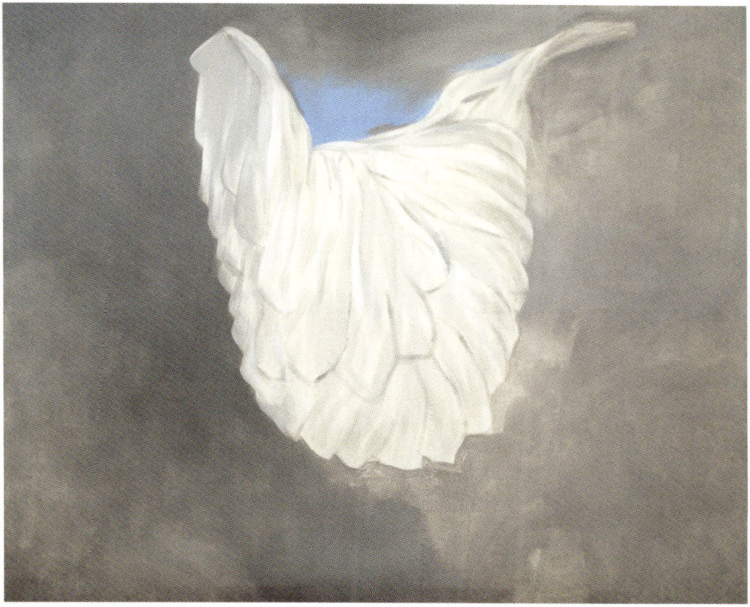

to see the empty tomb and Christ resurrected. All the greater was my surprise when the artist, talking about this canvas, the composition of which consists of the most economical colour fragments on a grey-and-white background, along with brush strokes concentrated in the upper half, observed: "I painted succinctly posed torn, wretched remnants of trees which appeared to be raised towards the heavens." As we see, upward movement can take on truly the most diverse terrestrial contexts, meanings and images!

Jan Merta, Big Purchase, 1993

The ability to link a fragment and the whole was probably most originally developed by Merta in his pictures focusing on weekend-cottage locations and slums. The fragments of paintings of cottages and chalets are diverse, encompassing typical depictions of a building with a tree in the foreground, views of the roofs of cottages from diverse angles, and dramatic images of structures that appear to be burning. Only after these scenes have been put together in the overall composition on a spatially free canvas can we begin to question the individual and overall meanings. Only on the basis of such an arrangement and the tension generated at the joints between the fragments can we ask about the actual purpose of the cottage, this symbol of modern man's vain escape from his urban existence.

What is the life of those who flee from their city apartment at the weekend, escaping to a rural cottage to indulge in the illusion of closeness to nature, but also fumbling for the greatest possible comfort and convenience? How much and what energy have they had to use to create a dwelling "in their own image"? With what kind of imagination did they work? And what about those people's perception of the term *home*, when they *dwell* in *dwellings* full of contradiction? How much do experiences of the socially concentrated environment of a high-rise differ from those of an area abundant in weekend cottages, or perhaps poor urban slums, where in India alone, for example, almost ten per cent of all the country's inhabitants live? And was the chalet not burnt down by its owner, always hastening forward in search of something, fleeing from something, and destroying everything around him just like Čapek's Prokop in *Krakatit*?

Here, somewhere in the tension between the fragments of chalets and their overall arrangement, the viewer is persistently filled with questions which stem from what Merta deliberately leaves unsaid in his pictures, and which must therefore necessarily be directed beyond them. The same questions occur to the audience when presented with Merta's portraits of specific individuals or directly ideal images of faces. With the extra-terrestrially conceived *Earthling* (1999) and the series *Ideal Radiant* (1996–2001), we do not have before us a cold art design of a certain type of face. We find ourselves viewing an image where we are no longer observing the colour of the eyes, the shape of the mouth

Jan Merta, Cottage (Red Bliss), 2009

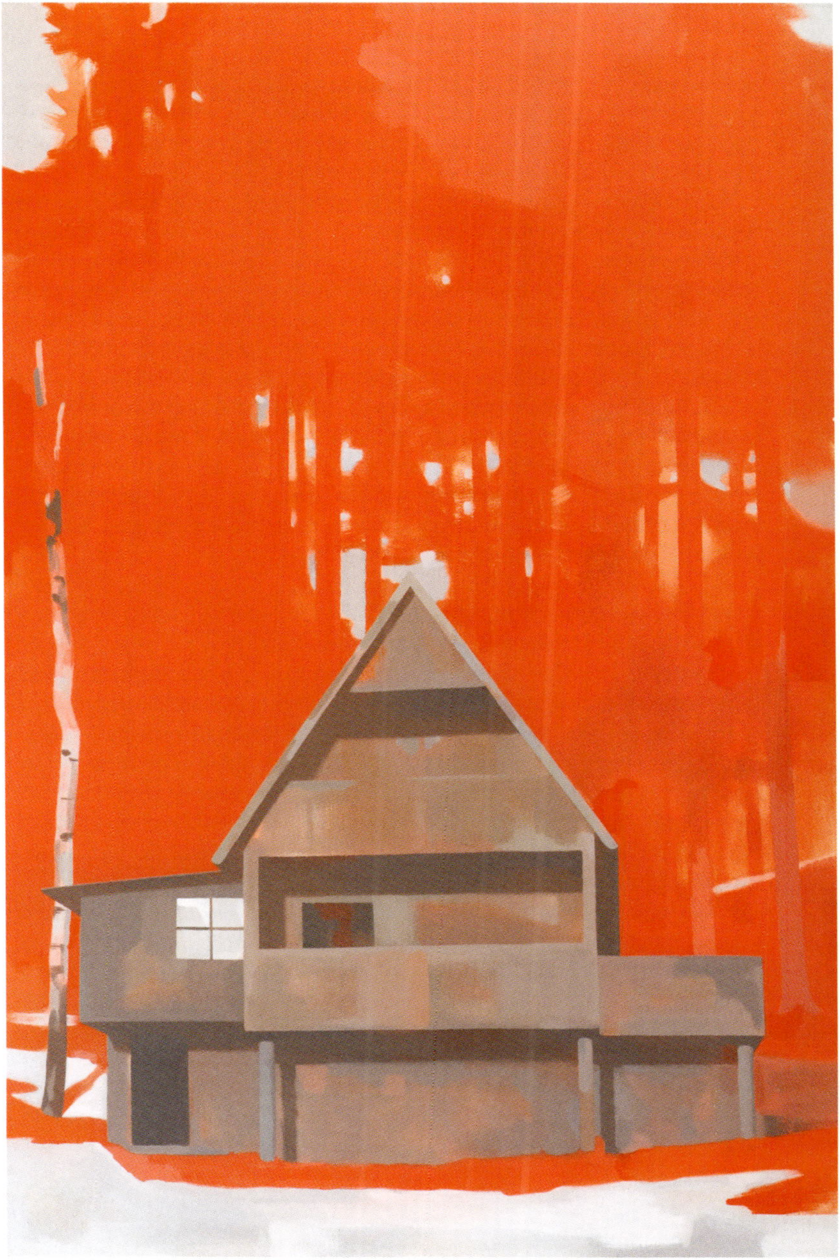

or the size and rounded nature of the nose. The view is direct, directly capturing the face in its vulnerability and nakedness, in which the whole universe is mirrored and through which, as the French philosopher Emmanuel Levinas claimed, we can see infinity.

According to Levinas, the face is not "seen". It is what cannot become a content, which your thought would embrace; it is uncontainable, it leads you beyond. Such a relationship to the face is then straightforwardly ethical and an examination of the face of the Other precedes any knowledge. According to Levinas, the Other, in this view, is always "higher" than me, is privileged in our relationship, and this is the source of our fundamental ethical responsibility for his life.

Likewise, Merta's wretched faces of child soldiers, graceful female faces or ideal radiant faces lead us "beyond" each image, the reality of the final world or human knowledge. They tell us that only in this encounter with infinite otherness do we explore ethics as the first means of finding our way around the world and its images, and of understanding both art and ourselves.

Yet it would be a gross mistake to regard Merta's work only as a serious ethical statement about the world and what precedes or transgresses it. It is also characterized by the above-mentioned caricature or detachment and irony. For example, the massive paintings of the monumental welding helmet (*To the Welders/Farewell, Master*, 2000) and grotesquely abstract object of climbing equipment (*To Mountain Climbers/Blue Velvet*, 1999–2000) are not only ambiguous in their names, but also extremely witty in the way they combine lightness with weight, a specific topic with an abstract depiction, and ultimately everyday banality with extraordinary mastery.

Jan Merta can afford such a grotesque gesture or frivolous topic because he is sure that, in his work, he is conveying something totally unique and original which can only be captured in the language of art and which is formed only in a supreme artistic act. Like the surrealists and, after them, so many other artists of innumerable directions and schools, he too goes beyond the boundaries of his own ego to create space for the free creative process and display it in all its most varied and richest forms. The modern canon of art as a communication of the incommunicable thus finds its own postmodern expression in Merta's work.

“DO YOU RECOGNIZE YOURSELVES?!”

THE ART OF UNREST IN MASS SOCIETY AND DIRECTNESS IN THE WORK OF JIŘÍ SURŮVKA

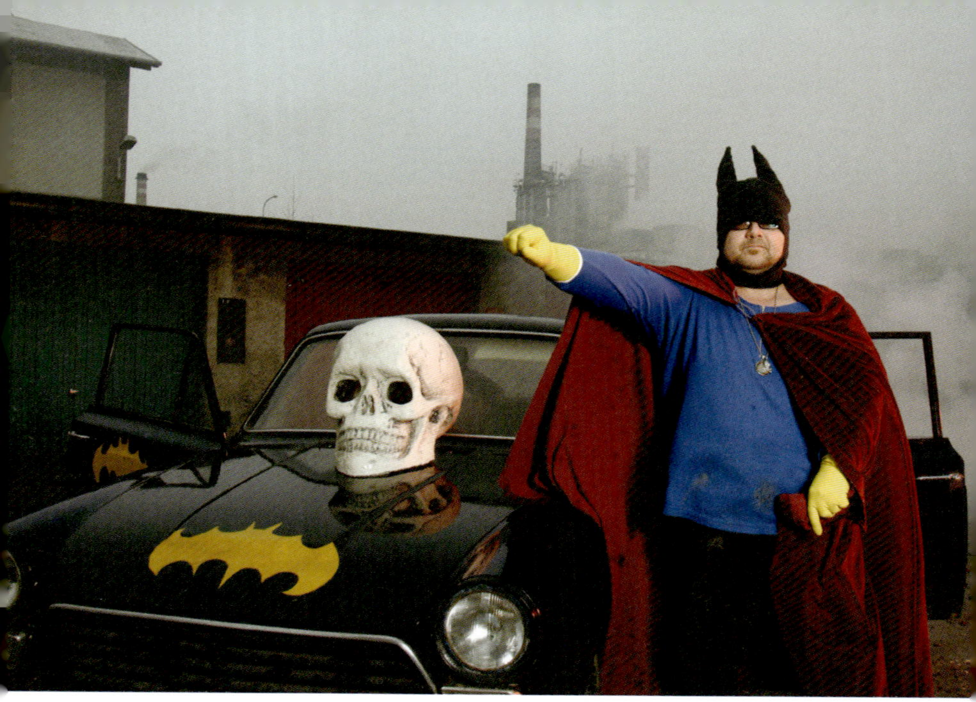

"Do You Recognize Yourselves?!"
The Art of Unrest in Mass Society and Directness in the Work of Jiří Surůvka

Ostrava embodies everything that Prague is missing, or what the capital tries hard to suppress. Prague brims with the confidence of a historical and cultural centre, without which the existence of Czech society in general would be unthinkable. Never mind that the Old Town Square has become a repulsive place of the basest forms of tourism, offering you bakers, blacksmiths and confectioners "in action" or rides around the old city centre, which increasingly resembles a Hollywood movie set. Although locals complain that the crystal-glass and souvenir shops are destroying the way their streets look, they still have a sense of exclusivity, even though their city increasingly brings to mind a historical carcass better viewed from a distance, or preferably only on a postcard.

In contrast, as soon as you arrive in Ostrava, you immediately get the feeling that you are not in Europe but in an American industrial agglomeration, through which various nations and ethnicities do not drift like some hedonistic tourists but, rather, in which they have lived and worked together for generations. Besides impressive buildings, you will also find ruins here; the city centre comes across as vague and suspicious, and everywhere you can feel the energy of people who have been attracted to this place by the desire for a more respectable, though cruelly gained, livelihood. As opposed to Prague, a fringe city which tries to present itself as the "Middle of Europe", Ostrava makes no attempt to mask its marginality and plebeian origin. Its wildness, ruggedness, transience and inflexibility makes it, in the words of Ludwig Wittgenstein, a quite distinct life form.

Naturally, completely different culture and art are born of such a form. The art community may be further away from Prague's publishing houses, theatres, galleries and curatorial offices, but this distance also releases creative energy and clarifies what is essential and what is still

Jiří Surůvka, Gotham City, 2009

worth doing in today's literature, music, visual art and drama. Telling examples of this are not only the existentially focused and disciplined stories of the recently deceased writer Jan Balabán or the poems of Petr Hruška, but also the visual and performance art of Jiří Surůvka.

Unlike most visual artists, Surůvka does not observe reality, but reads and then rewrites it in his paintings and collages, or plays it out in his performances and cabaret with his cousin Petr Lysáček in

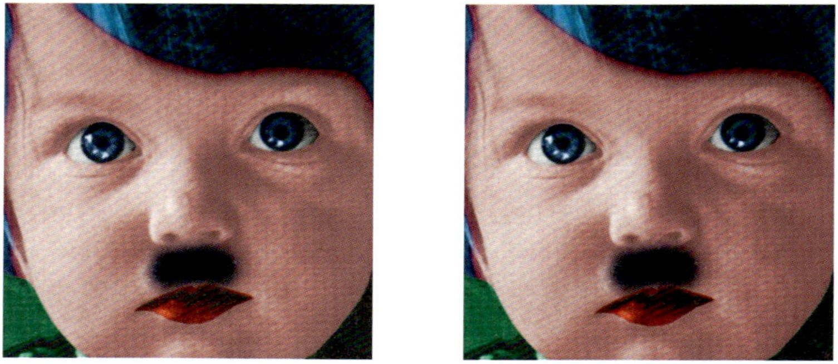

Lozinski Support Band, in the cabaret *Return of the Maestros*, or in other projects. The meaning, milieu and context are always more important to him than the image itself. In this respect, Surůvka is close to dadaist exuberance and spectacular provocation, aimed not only against social conventions, but just as much against art and the way it is run.

This basis is already apparent in his early *Iron Age* paintings (1987–1993), on which Surůvka collaborated with Lysáček, and in his *Paderlík and Death* from the mid-1990s, in which he placed not a romantic depiction of the expected "girl", but a puppet of a soldier-painter, embodying the state of visual arts and academic education in socialist Czechoslovakia. As also shown by later paintings with the classic themes *Death of Marat* (1998) and *Girl with the Head of Medusa* (1998), he is interested in far more than just superficial provocation with a simple critical subtext. In these and other images, we see a much more complicated aesthetic expression, in which liberating

Jiří Surůvka, Twins, 1997

laughter returns as a terrifying echo and a classic theme is illustrated with coarse, even brutal, brush strokes. Surůvka's artistic language has thus always teetered between "wild painting", inspired by the German *Die Junge Wilde* or Italian transavantgarde artists, and pop-art in all its descriptiveness, comic illustration and penchant for artistic and social references.

Nevertheless, Jiří Surůvka entered the broader public consciousness with his collage of a small child's face with Hitler's forelock and moustache, which he conceived in 1997 as a series of two computer airbrushed pictures and exhibited under the title *Twins*. The detailed depiction of the child's face here is not at all natural, instead creating a synthetic and aseptic impression. The Aryan blue eyes look more like those of the blinking dolls made in the former East Germany, and the mouth is covered with sharp red, computer cut-out lips. Inserted into this inhuman face of a child is a hairstyle with a typically low left forelock, transitioning from cobalt to raven, and, in particular, a half-blurry black mark under the nose, which might be a streak of dirt, but in this context will immediately be associated by everyone with Adolf Hitler's characteristic toothbrush moustache.

In this context, one is immediately tempted to compare Surůvka's work with Duchamp's classic portrait of a bearded *Mona Lisa* from 1919. Yet even a cursory glance should be enough to highlight a significant difference between the absolute abandon and provocativeness of Duchamp's dadaist "portrait" and Surůvka's vehemence, healthy anger and the directness with which he chooses political themes and iconic images that both immediately shocked and deeply troubled us.

Duchamp's *Mona Lisa* was meant as a provocation and mockery of the then prevailing art canon. Even so, this spirit of artistic and social rebellion contained a special naivety and playfulness, which, indeed, was always inherently a part of Dada. Duchamp's Mona Lisa is a joke and subversion, banality requiring courage and audacity to exhibit, as an original work, a classic portrait on which the artist has committed that most unoriginal of teenage acts, the scribbling of a beard on the face of Leonardo's ideal and mysterious beauty. All subsequent interpretations, such as the fact that the whiskers pointed to Leonardo's alleged homosexuality, are just superfluous additions to the initial provocative gesture.

In contrast, Surůvka's *Twins* is a thorough inversion of Duchamp's process. Although people are generally moved by the child's face just as stupidly as many a visitor to the Louvre admires the portrait of *Mona Lisa*, at first glance it is obvious that there is no moustache like a true moustache. The doubling of Surůvka's collage, a technique used at the same time by the artist in, for example, the airbrushed portraits *Good Boys* (1998) and *Bad Girls* (1998), goes far beyond the semantic field of provocation and forces viewers to ask who the twins are actually meant to be. Are they these two computer-cloned portraits? And who is their father? What is generally identical to the twins and what are we to imagine under their relationship? And in this case is it not the common symbolic power of opposites which we generally associate with the face of Adolf Hitler and a small child?

Duchamp's moustache is provocative and mocks the dying bourgeois world and its cultural illusions that had just collapsed in the turmoil of the First World War. In contrast, Surůvka is much more rigorous and views artistic provocation as a politically symbolic act attacking the society in which the bourgeoisie has long ceased to reign, having given way to the masses. His main target is the herd mentality and mass taste, with its obsessive imagery. The masses have encompassed not only politics or pop culture, but also sport, which is why Surůvka has composed airbrushed collages such as *Russian Ice-hockey Team* (1998) and the *German Ice-hockey Team* (1998), where the heads of Hitler and Stalin and their closest associates are superimposed on historical photographs of the sports teams. Whereas the dadaists were looking into the future when they mocked the prevailing conventions, Surůvka's post-dadaist political vision of the world is often directed into the past, a place where all kinds of nightmares are hunted.

Yet a computer collage of a child's face together with an iconic hairstyle and moustache inherently associated with the disaster of war, political collapse and the horrors of "civilized" Europe also contains, in itself, an intrinsic aesthetic and political logic. After all, Adolf Hitler liked to be photographed and filmed with young children,

Jiří Surůvka, The Scream, 1996

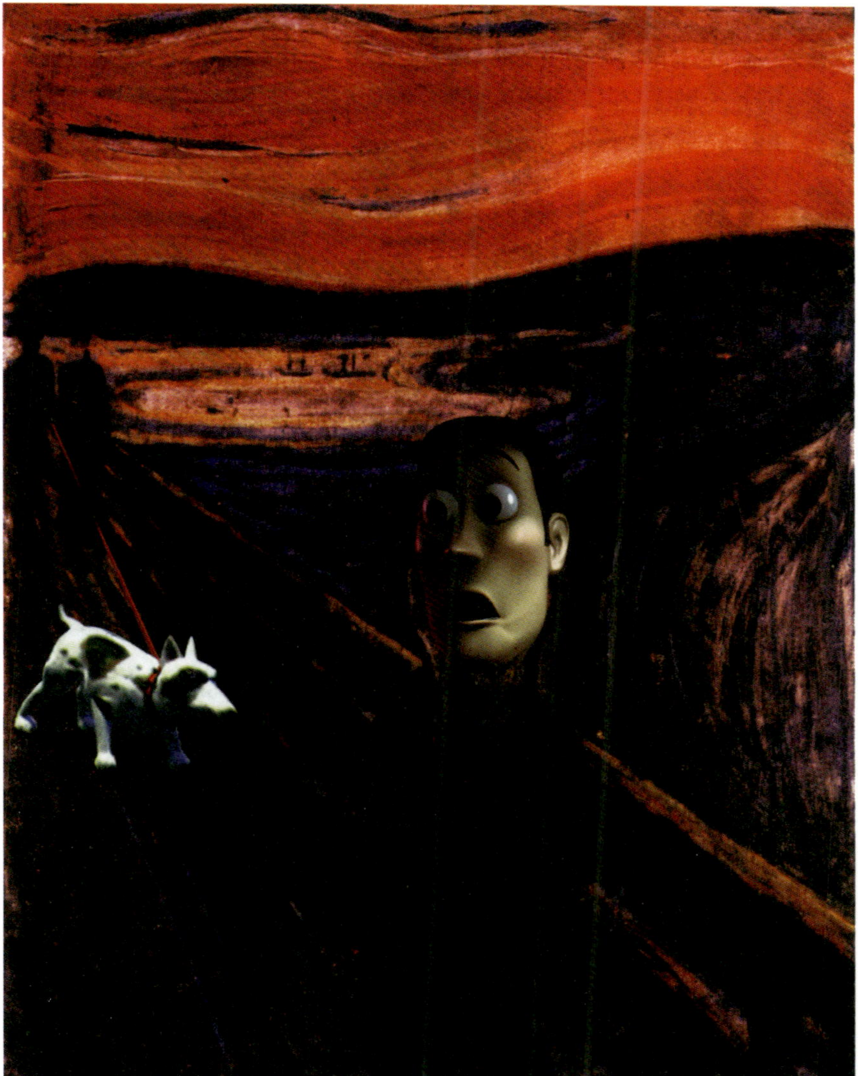

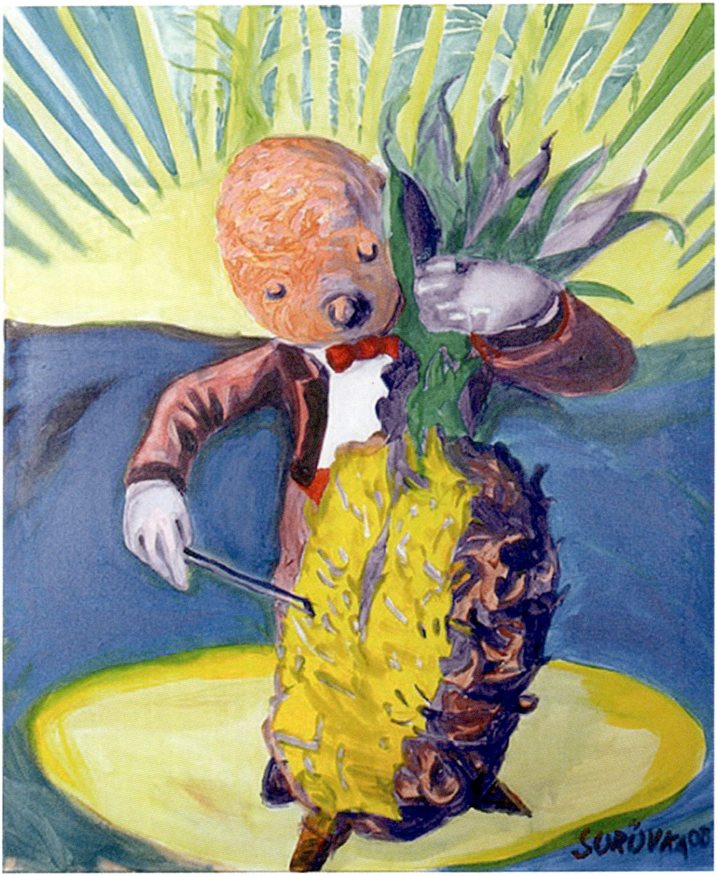

and poignant images of Aryan toddlers were skilfully exploited by the Nazi propaganda machine. Surůvka's computer airbrushing is perhaps ultimately the most realistic depiction of National Socialism. As if only the digital era in which we live and the computers we use in our daily lives have enabled us to see the true scope and enormity of political and propagandistic manipulation, which are far from unique to Nazi and Stalinist ideology.

Jiří Surůvka intensively examines the common basis, various ties and mutual influence of political and cultural clichés and manipulation in mass society. The targets of his visual interventions and subversions are therefore not only politics, but also contemporary pop culture and art in general. In this light, Disney characters appear in the middle of Munch's *The Scream* (1996), and photographs of old people's ugly faces are inserted into Warhol's iconic self-portraits and portraits of Marilyn Monroe. The artist very aptly termed these images *Marilyn Monroe in her Entirety* (1997) and *Andy W. in his Entirety* (2002).

An absurd gesture towards the icons of the culture industry is also reflected, with extraordinary power, in a gynaecological chair occupied by a tubby figure with a typical Batman mask, holding before him his newborn child, a tiny Batman. This monochromatic sculpture, *Fatherhood*, from 2003, which is a monumental variation on pop-art aesthetics and its suicidal narcissism, remains one of Surůvka's landmark works, in which the pop-art sense of banality perfectly complements its ironic revelation and where absurd gestures often simply emphasize even more absurd tragedy.

It is this general creative approach that guided Surůvka towards what is probably his most significant and long-term cycle, *Masters of War* (1996 to 2008), which he created in parallel as a series of computer airbrushed and painted canvases. On one of the paintings, a figure sits on a chair in the foreground in evening dress, his head a pear, and plays a sliced pear with his bow while a bomber flies overhead in the background. In another painting, a figure with the head of a bunch of grapes conducts while a group of prisoners from a concentration camp, with their hands up, walks towards him. On another canvas, a tubby figure with the head of a plum blows a trumpet while, in the background, the bombed-out ruins of a city burn. Similarly, a pineapple-head uses a sliced pineapple as a bass, while behind him we see the glow of a nuclear explosion. And Mr Onion blithely plays an organ of asparagus while the image is shrouded in the smoke of one of the recent fires of war somewhere in the Middle Eastern desert.

Jiří Surůvka , Pineapple (from the series Masters of War), 2008

Society wants fun and feasting even while it witnesses its own tragedy. Tragedy becomes slapstick, slapstick tragedy. Batman bombs Kabul, contemporary German politicians hold spades, smiling at the entrance gate to a concentration camp with the inscription "Arbeit Macht Frei", Bill Clinton looks like he has come from Alien Nation, and spotted cows, painted in military camouflage colours, graze in the Sudetenland. No, Jiří Surůvka is certainly no moralist; for that, he is too honest a Dada artist who *knows no taboo* in his work. Like no one else, he has taken the liberty of using well-known photographs of the gaunt bodies of victims from concentration camps, replacing their heads with lemon and cabbage, and making them into new characters parodying the famous British duo of artists Gilbert and George. The artist was shielded from scandal only by his talent and ability to use open provocation within a much more complicated creative approach that might be dubbed *art of unrest*.

Surůvka also likes apocalyptically edgy images, the character of which he immediately disparages with Dadaist effervescence, such as *Ground Zero* from 2002, where, from the perspective of a person weighing himself, we see two hairy legs standing on bathroom scales, while the needle points to zero weight. In his giant nine-metre computer airbrushed *Strict God* (1999–2000), the artist has used monumental frescos from the Sistine Chapel. In one illustration, in which Michelangelo originally captured the moment when the stars and planets were created, Surůvka inserts a whip into the Creator's hand, while in another shows Him throwing bombs at the ground. In this case, this is no longer a happening of apocalyptic horsemen, in which Surůvka participated in the mid-1990s, but an apocalyptic image of the inseparability of creation from destruction, birth from extinction.

Yet is this airbrushed work not the most supreme manifestation of Surůvka's absurd humour? After all, associating Armageddon with something so humanly stupid and brutal as industrially produced bombs is itself a manifestation of the greatest absurdity. Walter Benjamin, in his essay *Critique of Violence*, wrote that, beyond the human mind, administering a realm of ends and means, there is divine violence, which reigns over "all life for the sake of the living". This is not some mythical bloody violence over mere life, based on a system of crimes and rewards for human acts and sacrifices to the gods, but violence surpassing human intellect, and manifested both through the victims and the reconciliation between God and man. The frightening images of apocalyptic horror we know from the history of Christian art, in which sinners are condemned for their acts to eternal damnation, would then be just an example of a fundamental misunderstanding of God who, for the salvation of man, even committed violence on himself.

This renders Surůvka's collage, in which God grasps the destructive creations of modern man, all the more important. Here, man imposes on God a form of punishment of humankind which is based entirely on human inventions and the capability of modern humanity to exterminate itself on an industrial scale. Surůvka has quite exceptionally managed to capture a key feature of politics, namely the masking of political terror with ideological or theological rigour. He has captured the fundamental transformation of modern civilization, which, as the German philosopher Peter Sloterdijk wrote, no longer wages conventional war in order to defuse the power of the enemy army, but all-out war to control the airspace and environment of an enemy society and to totally destroy it with this terror. Ever since the German army, in Ypres in 1915, used the first ever weapon of mass destruction – poisonous gas, humankind has not been engaged in wars, but in terrorist extermination campaigns of unprecedented proportions, which, like the Nazi extermination of Jews in gas chambers, surpass all apocalyptic imagery of Renaissance maestros in terms of horror and industrial organization.

Jiří Surůvka's work also confirms, *inter alia*, that in principle there are three types of artists. The first type constantly measures itself against eternity and strives, with its work, to come as close as possible to eternity. For these artists, art is a transgression, an overlap of fleeting everyday life, if not religious experience, and a celebration of what is eternal and what outlives human life. The second type, in contrast, holds in contempt such artistic gestures intent on eternity as undue pomp and posturing, juxtaposing this with civil art of the everyday and the immediate experience as the fundamental basis of all art. These artists value sincerity and authenticity more than style and the starting point of all their efforts is the challenge "Know Thyself!" from the Temple of Apollo in Delphi. For artists of this type, art becomes a special form of diary, self-exploration and constant examination of the self, which the artist wants to share with the reader, listener or viewer.

Besides these two types, there is another, third type, which does not aim to capture eternity or share the authenticity of its own experiences, but which is most happy constantly communicating with viewers, listeners or readers. It is as though, through their work, these artists are primarily asking "Do you recognize yourself?". Today, among artists of this type in Czech visual art, Jiří Surůvka excels for his ability to directly and provocatively express himself while asking deep and fundamental questions about our present existence.

Surůvka's directness is a reaction to a culture in which life is lived quickly, and therefore it is necessary to express oneself fast and clearly. If you want to convey what is essential, you must not waste time with sophisticated aesthetic gestures which would attract, at most, critical aesthetes and gallery snobs. There is no time; we need to cut to the chase. Moreover, this is precisely what the philosopher and phenomenologist Edmund Husserl was advocating at the time Marcel Duchamp appended a moustache and beard to the Mona Lisa. In our late times, it is not enough for art to provoke and punch us in the nose. It must also shake our heads wildly so that we recognize what is around us and what is happening with us. It would be difficult to find anyone here today who is more capable of this than Jiří Surůvka.

STARRY SKY ABOVE ME, IDEAL IMAGE WITHIN ME

ANTONÍN STŘÍŽEK'S "HEDGEHOG" PAINTING

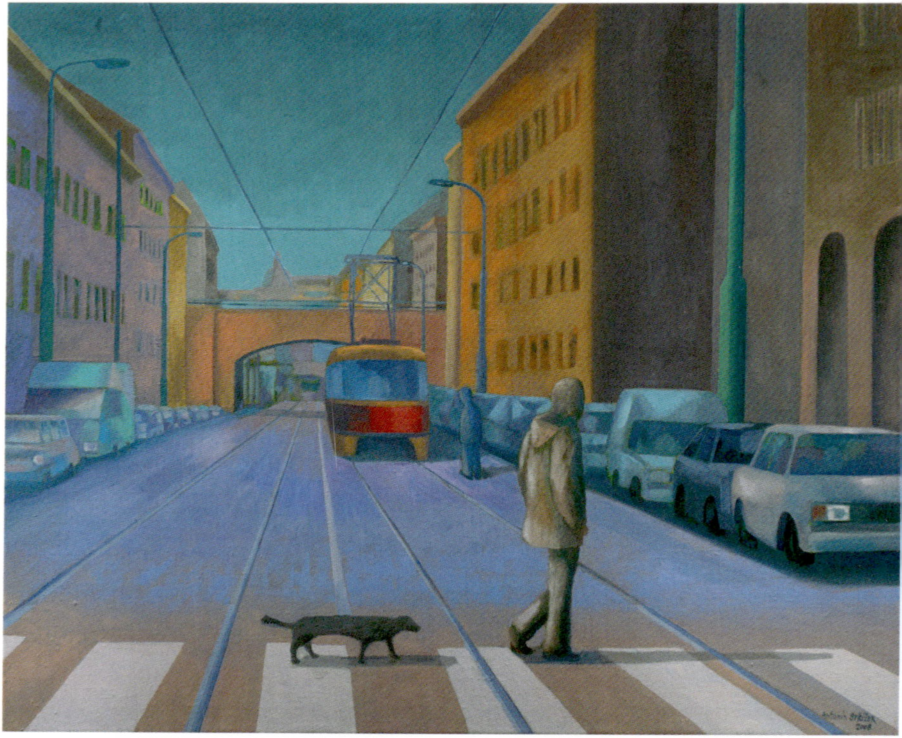

Starry Sky above Me, Ideal Image within Me
Antonín Střížek's "Hedgehog" Painting

If you visit Prague's Centre for Theoretical Studies, that unique crossroads in the Czech academic and intellectual landscape, you will encounter many interesting people from different disciplines, as well as philosophers, writers and the most diverse eccentrics in the best sense of the word. This community, with roots stretching back to dissident seminars held in homes, has expanded, converged with official science, and regularly invites top domestic and foreign guests to lecture. What is more, the CTS is a place where you can come across pictures whose depth of thought runs parallel to the lecture series or publications on offer. Standing out among them is the most philosophical image of Czech postmodern painting, by Antonín Střížek.

Painted on the canvas are two wild geese standing at the edge of a cliff, the sea extending before them far into the distance, as they look up to the sky – two-legged animals, like people, but also endowed with wings and the ability to fly, that age-old human desire. What is more, in the geese's eyes there is a peculiar expression, as though reflecting that Kantian "starry sky above me" and its inseparable "moral law within me". Yet this is no superficial caricature or ridicule of man, whose yearning has been at least partially succoured in our technological age as he is lifted into the air in "flying machines", while his soul is dragged through brutalities intended to fill the void following the abandonment of the categorical imperative. The earth and space captured in the painting do not set off one creature against another; rather, they make the geese a companion of man.

The firmament spreads over us and the rest of creation, and in today's fragile world, on the brink of ecological disaster, we know that moral law cannot segregate man from animate and inanimate nature,

Antonín Střížek, Karlín, 2008

but, rather, must bond him with it. After all, the geese are much closer to heaven than people, even though people, with their technological inventions and knowledge, get carried away by the illusion that they eventually will be all-pervasive.

The wild geese do not have the dignity of aristocratic swans, so Zeus would certainly not have selected this form to lie with Leda. Those painted by Střížek would clearly have paid more attention to the fall of Icarus than the peasant in Bruegel's famous painting, who continues ploughing indifferently while the tragedy of the son plummeting into the sea with warped artificial wings plays out nearby. Will not we, in our collapsing world, ultimately engender more sympathy in those who, according to cold Cartesian intellect, should have absolutely no emotion or intelligence? Was there not more sense in St Francis's reading of the Bible to animals? And is not our modern technological era challenged by the "goose question" of Střížek's work, which we might sum up as: "Why do you want to fly, man, when you have sprouted no wings?" What actually is naturalness and what role does human nature play in it?

There is only one image, but countless depictions. No other artist today is able to express creative tension between the image and its depiction as strongly as Antonín Střížek. While the image is the ideal we carry in our heads, its actual depiction will always vary according to our momentary mood, experience or hindsight. Even though art stands or falls on skill and the talent of depiction, without the elemental force of the ideal image, which is close yet unavailable, no such art could exist.

Střížek's images are what, with a healthy dose of hyperbole, we might paradoxically describe as *postmodern artistic Platonism*. They are based on idealized forms rather than realistic detail. The silhouettes of buildings thus transitioned smoothly into abstract shapes, the simple beauty of a curve and primary colours radiate from neon lights, artificial compositions of three-dimensional geometric objects have an atmosphere of specific still lives. The importance of the subject gives way to inner formal tension, whether the diverse penetration of light, colour contrasts or contradictions between the capture of movement and immobile situations on city streets.

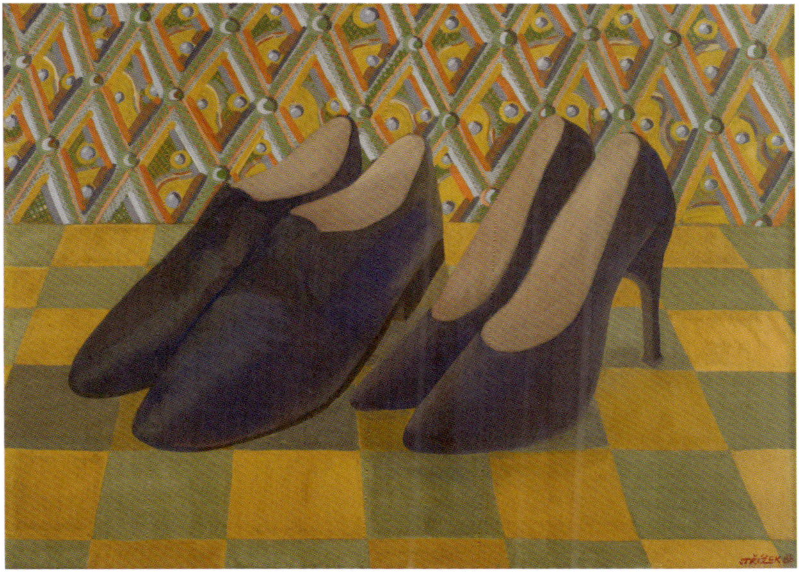

It is as though, despite all the idealism, Střížek's images were also guided by the famous work of the American philosopher Richard Rorty, *Philosophy and the Mirror of Nature*, in which the author also recommends that we abandon the illusion that it is possible to have direct insight into the world of nature and that all we need to do is properly clean the mirror in which we are to see the world! According to Rorty, philosophy should instead concentrate on what constitutes it, namely its language, metaphors and the arsenals of dictionaries it uses to construct images of our reality and also – as we know from experience – constantly change them. The history of philosophy and thought in general is not a history of the refinement of the image of the world, but a constantly repeated and challenged attempt at the most faithful possible depiction thereof.

Antonín Střížek, Shoes, 1988

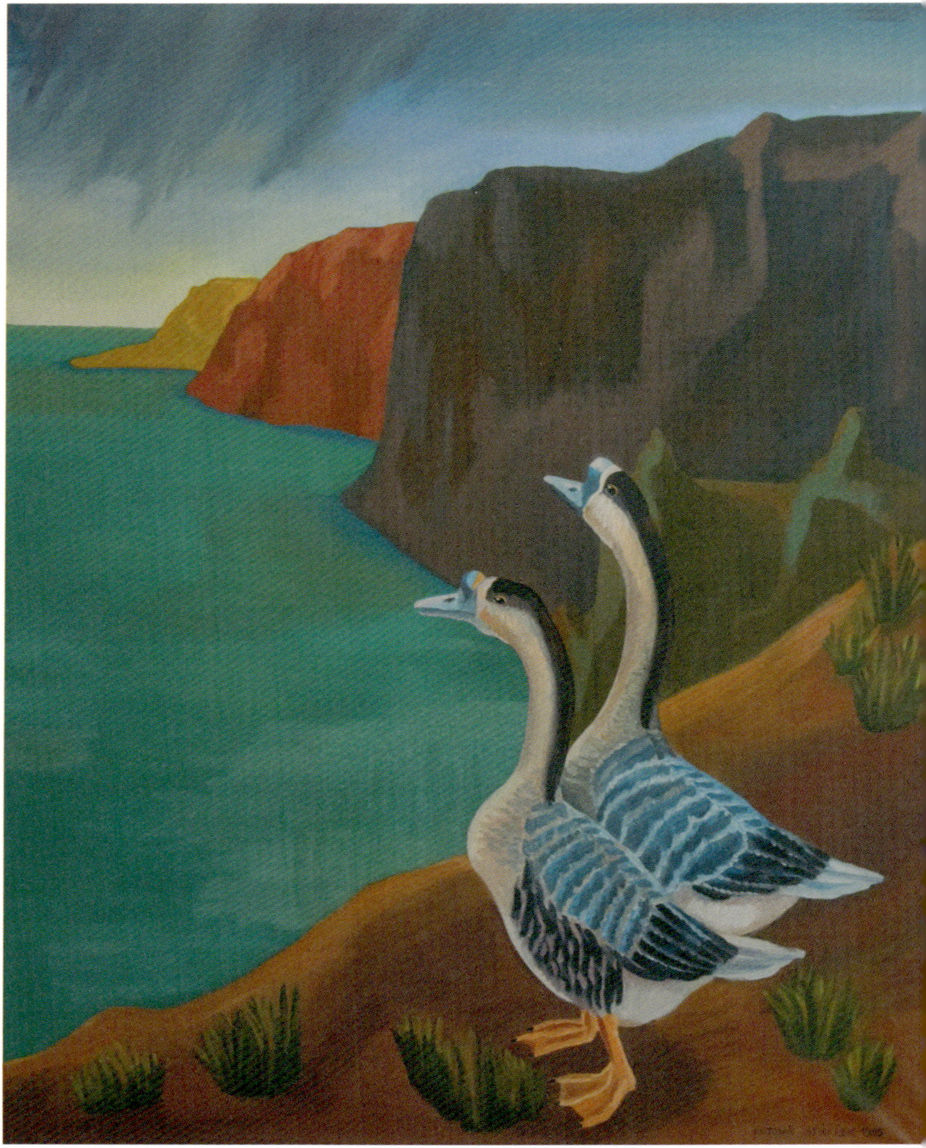

Střížek's depiction of ideal art forms in specific scenes of everyday reality is unique on the Czech art scene. Although no painter of his generation is as strongly influenced by romanticism as he is, it would be a big mistake to view Střížek's canvases as a mere manifestation of some sort of postmodern romantic idyll. While Caspar David Friedrich and other Romantics admired by the painter combined the language of large symbols with individual experience and the absolute pre-eminence of authentic self-expression, Střížek primarily addresses the internal structure and characteristics of a work rather than its outer descriptiveness, psychologization or social context.

In this respect, his approach is clearly formalist. This is particularly apparent in the large romantic citations attained by Střížek in his landscape painting. Even here, for example, the energy of abstract painting radiates from a line of trees. The romantic idyll is challenged in his pictures even though they are full of romanticizing and sometimes even melancholic scenes. We would search in vain here for a sense of romantic wonder or any sensory and emotional harmony because the artist has set himself the critical task of exploring the very conditions under which the image forms such an idyll in the viewer.

Střížek's images are thus a study of the possibilities of idyllic construction, which in itself precludes our perception of them merely in a superficially idyllic effect. They are meta-images that become their own problems. They completely lack the romantic ethos of the spiritual movement, in which the artist assumes the role previously played, as argued, for example by Walt Whitman in his time, by the priest, i.e. the role of a spiritual leader guiding readers, listeners and viewers to an insight into the true state of the world and their own souls. There is no place here for the romantic notion of the artist as a creature walking in God's footsteps thanks to his ability to create new worlds and, as such, leading the way for other mortals.

In Střížek's work, the only possible leader is the viewer herself, not the artist, who wishes to assume the position of a sort of "shepherd of beings". Střížek's expression is too civilist for that. He shares with the Romantics a respect for symbolic expression, and also has an affinity towards the desire for authenticity, but realizes that he must embark on this quest from the opposite side, i.e. by capturing everyday life in

Antonín Střížek, Wild Geese, 1989

its commonplaceness, bereft of questionability.

It is from this apparent slowness and banality of everyday life, moreover, that the most telling ideal images of the world that surrounds us and in which we live can be formed. Furthermore, the ability to construct and store such an image in one's mind, is by no means limited to romantic artists in a mystical trance. Here, for example, we might draw on the evolutionary theory espoused by Charles Darwin, who delighted in proclaiming himself an ignorant with respect to any arts and denounced contemporary art as a waste of money and time. When John Ruskin showed him his private collection of Turner's paintings, Darwin reportedly said that he could not understand what the famous critic saw in them. And yet, when we consider Darwin's career as a scientist, we cannot but arrive at the conclusion that, in the absence of imagination and immense sensitivity to the diversity of forms and contexture of his study material, our image of animate and inanimate nature today would be much different.

Would evolutionary theory have been possible if Turner or Friedrich had not elucidated the uniqueness of imagination to the human mind? Is there any difference between the imagination of scientists and artists? And what connects them both, for example, with the capacity of a simple man to recall memories of past events and metaphorically reconstruct them in his mind?

Like Tomáš Císařovský, his colleague from the same generation, Antonín Střížek is intrigued by the past and its reconstruction. Unlike Císařovský, whose pictorial cycles are based on epicness and constant communication between the social and cultural present and past, Střížek works with images of the past by asking what happened to our sensory perception between the past and the present. The critical factor is not, then, an artistic retelling of our history, but the secret of the *interval*, i.e. the time elapsed between past and present experience, the setting for that which Střížek particularly wants to capture – our shift in the perception of the past and its pictorial reconstitution.

We are thus witnesses to a peculiar artistic recursion of history in which the search for the meaning of the past is replaced by the issue

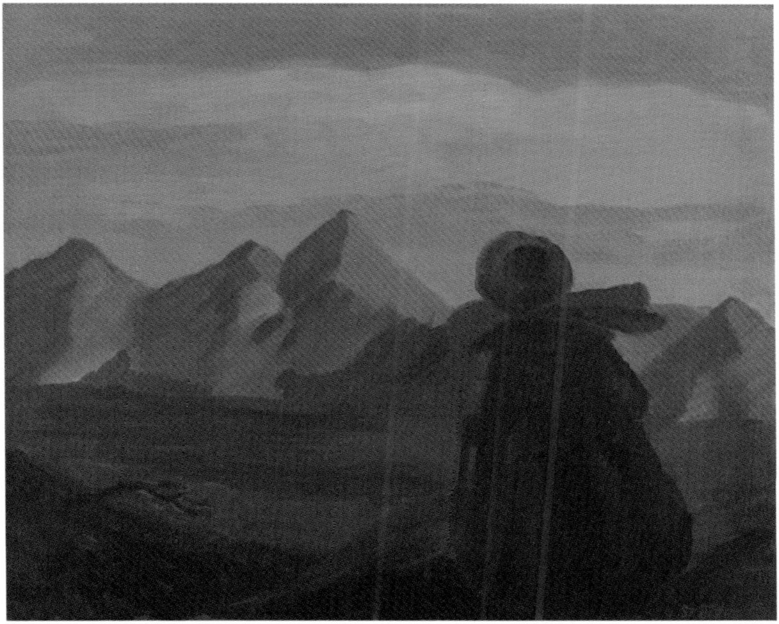

of how the past changes under the influence of the present and our perception. This is perhaps most noticeable in those visual cycles in which Střížek is inspired by the civilist poetry of Group 42 (*Skupina 42*), the members of which, in the 1940s, discovered the beauty of the urban fringes, nocturnal streets and pedestrians, cars and other vehicles, technical inventions and structures such as gas holders and water tanks.

What the painters František Gross, František Hudeček, Jan Smetana and Kamil Lhoták considered the civilist beauty of the fringes, where the familiarity of the moment meets the constructivist pathos of technique, is reconstructed by Střížek into images where the banality of everyday life and aesthetic civilism become distinctive features lacking direct ties to current or past reality. We cannot say here: "How beautiful it used to be!" or "How nice it would be if it was as it used to be!" Again, these are

Antonín Střížek, Mácha, 1989

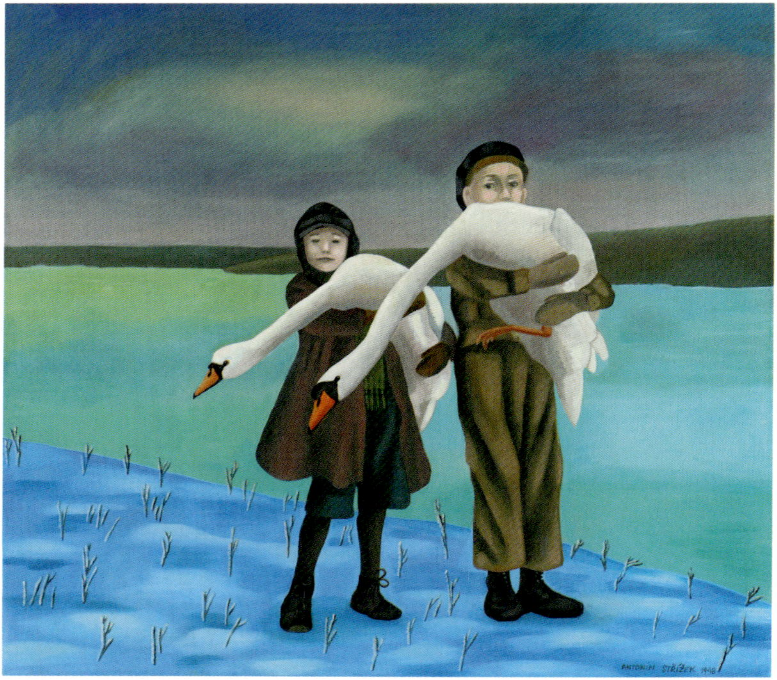

meta-images in which the civilist poetry of one of the most important artistic groups of the last century itself becomes a symbol and object of aesthetic study by the artist today.

Symbols become banality and the banality of the everyday becomes symbols. In Střížek's work, civilism is partially romanticized, but only in the form of a reconstructed citation of past artistic trends, their poetry or the overall period to which those trends belong and in which they were shaped. The same can be said, of course, of Střížek's reconstruction of our everyday lives. Subjects that in our lives are so present that we do not even notice them are relieved of the burden of their utility value by the painter in his pictures; he explores them as individual human creations and aestheticizes the environment in which

Antonín Střížek, Boys with Swans, 1998

they are found. As such, individual paintings capture, in objectivity, for example, the cups and glasses from which we drink or plain old cardboard egg boxes we see at home whenever we open the fridge.

Likewise, we do not notice those fire extinguishers in all the corners of public buildings, but in his depiction of them Střížek introduces sophisticated compositional play with light and colour contrasts. These are, in fact, also typical for his series of paintings of contemporary cities. For example, a woman on the phone, her dress and figure glowing in the same shades of green as the parked car she is walking past, makes her way down Myslíkova Street in Prague, which is drenched in the evening sun. The much worn metaphor of shade, which, according to the usual clichés, "we all drag around with us" and which is generally "a shadow of the past", becomes the focal point of the whole picture, but it is in front of the woman and she is staring at it as she walks. Is this the shadow of the future from which there is no escape? And why is her vague figure so convulsive, and with whom and about what can she be talking at this time, when it is clearly getting late and the street is emptying? And what are we to make of the man who, in another painting, is crossing the road on a pedestrian crossing in the early morning, with a lightness of step and a dog at his heels, as he watches a tram moving away down a street in the Karlín district of Prague. Is the melancholic mood the result of the colour scheme, or is it formed by tension between the vehicle travelling along the rails according to a precise timetable and the free, ambling gait of the man and his dog? Yes, symbolism may be the greatest banality and banality may, just as easily, be an eminent symbol.

When, more than half a century ago, the British-Latvian philosopher Isaiah Berlin published *The Hedgehog and the Fox*, he incorporated a fragment attributed to the Greek poet Archilochus: "The fox knows many little things, but the hedgehog knows one big thing." This expression inspired Berlin, with his typical wit and bravado, to divide important thinkers and artists of our civilization into foxes and hedgehogs. The group of hedgehogs included Plato, Pascal, and Hegel, as well as Dostoyevsky, Nietzsche and Proust. In contrast, according to Berlin the foxes comprise not only Aristotle, but also Erasmus,

Montaigne, Goethe, Tolstoy, and, of course, the big fox William Shakespeare.

In this context, it was as though the history of Western thought and culture consisted of the constant complementarity of hedgehogs and foxes. Without Plato, we would not have Aristotle, without Montaigne's essays we would judge Pascal's ideas differently, and the history of the modern novel would remain incomprehensible to us if we had not grasped the fundamental differences between the ways in which Dostoyevsky and Tolstoy wrote.

This division of prominent figures would have remained mere social entertainment if Berlin had not developed the key idea that in everyone, philosopher or artist, there is constant strife between the characteristics of a hedgehog and a fox. Berlin claims, for example, that Tolstoy had the talents of a fox, but spent his whole life wishing he was a hedgehog. If we allow ourselves to be drawn into Berlin's classification game, we could similarly conclude that, for example, Nietzsche also wanted, in his post-romantic gestures, to break, sly as a fox, into the realm of exact "gay" science. Finally, Berlin himself, like a fox, brought various thinkers into his burrow of essays in order to demonstrate on them the hedgehog's big and important idea that the modern period did not begin until romanticism because it conceals an ambivalent shift towards personal freedom and total denial of such freedom in the name of nationalist and other collectivist ideologies.

I admit that, on reading Berlin's essay and considering Archilochus's fragment, I immediately thought how this division could be applied to contemporary Czech art. Besides the foxes constantly running around, such as Jiří David and Petr Nikl, it has also been significantly shaped in the past two decades by hedgehogs, among whom Antonín Střížek stands out by painting his ideal image again and again, with almost oriental passion and patience. Yet, with the sharp-wittedness of the fox, he exploits various art forms to get as close as possible to his image. In other words, he is constantly enraptured by the ideal image with the concentration of the hedgehog, even though his fox experience sceptically says that he can always only depict it, but never directly capture or express it. As we can see, the discord between the hedgehog and the fox in each of us has not only literary or philosophical, but, also, quite specific and distinctive art forms.

FULLNESS, PLURALITY AND INNER FREEDOM

JIŘÍ PŘIBÁŇ
AN INTERVIEW WITH IVAN MEČL FOR THE UMĚLEC MAGAZINE

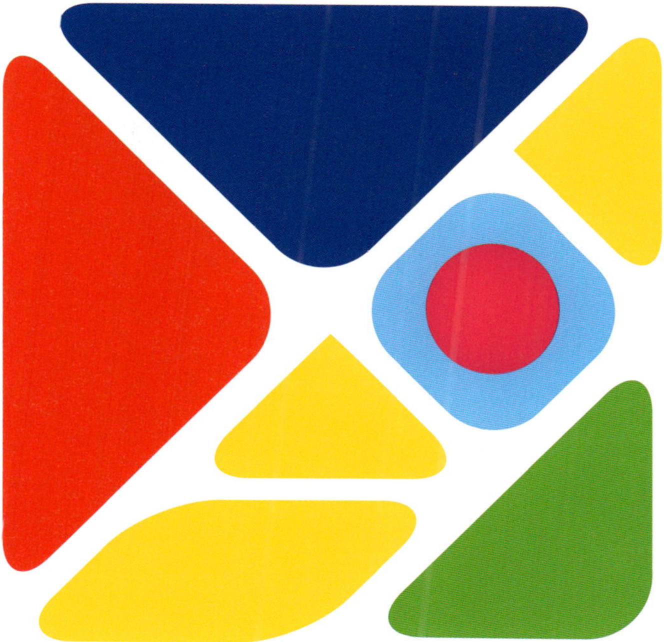

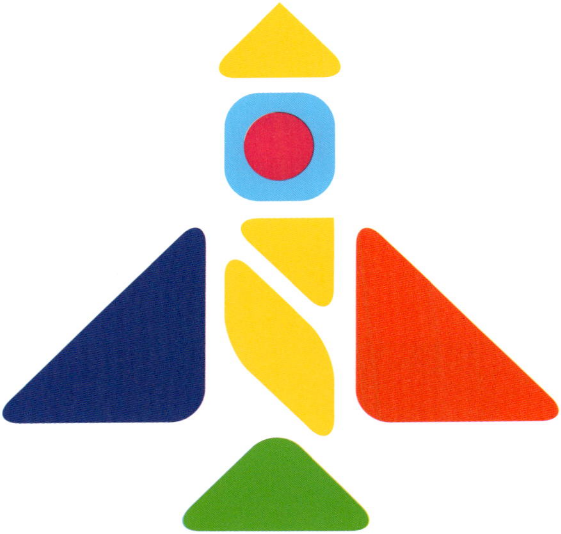

Fullness, Plurality and Inner Freedom

An Interview with Ivan Mečl for the Umělec Magazine

I reckon you've noticed that the number of artists has multiplied by hundreds in the past thirty years. It's easy to notice at collective exhibitions, or the number of authors that take part in exchange programs. Holland and Germany seem to almost mass-produce their artists... Do you think that this is the materialization of the avant-garde's dream? At the beginning of the last century they said that in the future everyone would be an artist.

I do not think that this is the materialization of the avant-garde's dream. It is moreover a reaction to today's complex society, no matter if we call it modern, or post-modern, liquid, empty, digital, instant, and so on. The metaphors that modern society makes up to describe or to better understand itself, quickly change and then disappear again. The determining attributes of this society are immense complexity and functionality. But even inside this more and more complicated society - where its individual systems (doesn't matter if it's economy, law, or science) cannot be fully understood by nonqualified common sense - every person keeps searching for an opportunity for self-understanding and self-creation. In other words, every person keeps looking for something that is special, individual, and authentic. Modern society then expects art to offer exactly this very opportunity. Art doesn't have to be true. But it always has to be real. That is the difference between art and science, for example.

The fact that a growing number of people are allowed to create - the massive support of art - might also be an answer to the unemployment question. Sophisticated prevention, how to please the critics, otherwise unneeded by society. Isn't it a good strategy to prevent the artist/intellectuals, that were the moving force of protests in the sixties, from flooding the streets again? There are enough reasons to do so: wars, poverty, ecology... But it doesn't seem to strike up enough interest. The potential "naughties" seem to be satiated.

We must separate the reason why a person chooses to become an artist, and the art business, i.e. the social support for contemporary art. It is true, that the grants, European funds etc., all of this creates a particular system of social goods redistribution, which of course brings certain control and dependence hazards. Art is then already led into particular canals, information flows, and social expectations beforehand.

Is it a good thing, that an intellectual is cultivated through grants? Thanks to this, one shall never become a leading element of social transmutations.

The thought that we could understand society as a whole, and thanks to this knowledge we could then commence to change society, is illusory. Every intellectual today knows, that he is moving in some kind of a context, and thus he is not in a prerogatived position of someone, who could describe and understand society in its totality and thus could become, as you call it, a leader of social transmutations. Foucault once referred to Sartre's philosophy as the last heroic attempt of an intellectual to describe 20th century society through 19th century language. Today's intellectuals are no longer the keepers of general intelligence and culture. Each and every one of them has become a specialist. Today's ideas aren't mediated by intellectuals, they are mediated by the internet. But Foucault still thoroughly engaged in the most diverse battles for social and political reforms from the title of his knowledge, no matter if the topics were psychiatric clinics, jails, or marginal minority support. If something from Foucault's work has still persisted a quarter of a century after his death, then it is above all the ability to lead an active resistance, and to confront the disciplinary techniques of modern society, which are becoming by far more cunning and dangerous. Because even an intellectual can be captive to these techniques. He has to apply for grants, summarize his publishing activities if he works at a university, or he is expected to express his views on public events in banal language through the media.

Don't you think that this multiplication could endanger the exclusivity of an artist? Maybe modernism didn't thoroughly think through what will actually happen, if this dream really comes true?

These are parallel processes. We have more opportunities and more control. The current society provides great opportunities for self-creation, and not only for artists. But nobody is taking advantage of these opportunities. A person has the potential for all sorts of activities, but a person is the happiest, when he is passive. At the same time the society creates these opportunities in such manner, that it can always have them under control. In sociology taking advantage of such opportunities is called adaptability to external conditions. Freedom is then understood as the ability to adapt to an

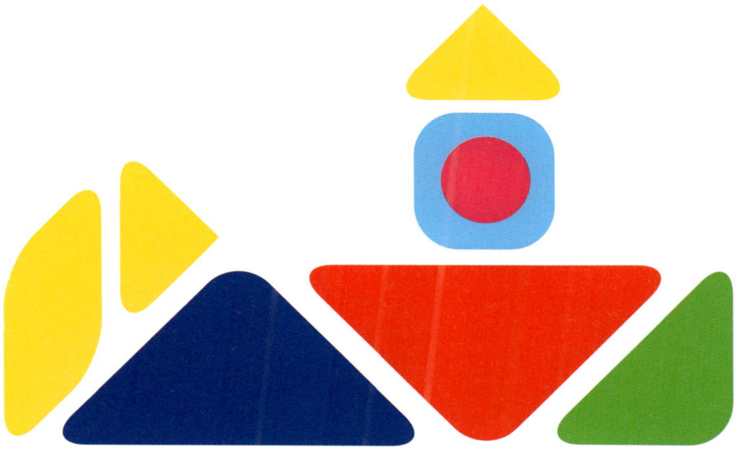

environment and make use of it for your own good. It has nothing to do with exclusivity.

Only in modern times is an artist expected to create something that shall be authentic, original, and exclusive in a certain way, under any conditions. The uniqueness of art resides in such a contradiction of social adaptation. The artistic truth is never absolute, but it always has to be personal and lived through. This expectation is what the avant-garde was basing its protests against social conventions upon. But we live in times where we don't have to ask what art should protest against at all. What's worth protesting in an evermore faster changing and unstable society? We have to ask, what opportunities exist for something we call engaged art? Thus today's art must be analytic, not utopian.

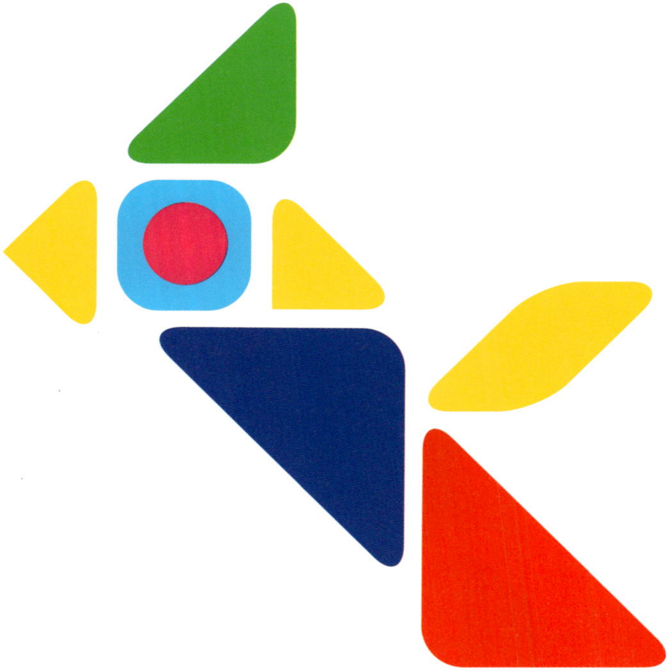

And isn't this just a romantic image of an artist? An artist was never a model of a moral personality. Mostly he or she was one of the most opportunistic and salable individuals.

You're right. Romanticism and the birth of modern society go hand in hand. Suddenly the artist is the bearer of genius, of collective soul - be it the soul of a certain nation or a soul of the whole world, reflected through art. As if the artist was asking herself questions on behalf of the common mortal. That is of course a very dangerous role. It lures one to think of the artist as of a conscience of humankind, the conscience of a nation, and as a conscience of a prophet. A prophet that tells the common mortal what to do and what not to. Authenticity hides very strong and tempting normative expectations.

Is art the last domain, where an author can let herself simplify, abbreviate, without passing off as awkward? On the intellectual field there is an ongoing anxiety from abbreviating. The authors mostly state beforehand that the whole problem is "of course much more complicated". Only in art it is possible to say: "No, it's not more complicated, it has been wrong since the beginning."

Well, that's dead on. Art is exactly a domain where humor, allusions, non-seriousness, and irony reign. You can understand something, which otherwise seems incomprehensible through a fragment, or an apparently marginal remark. Art actually brings us back to reality.

But is that a good thing that it has stayed this way only in art?

This is for sure the function of art in society. And thanks to this a lot of people today create art, rather than looking at it, listening to it, or reading it. There exists a need to do something, but there is also the need to understand reality, which seemingly stays trapped in the hands of expert knowledge. Self-creation and self-understanding go hand in hand with the much more common need to understand the surrounding environment and to reorganize it. There is the need to do something and on the other hand there is the contemporary art business that lacks the sex appeal of classic modernism. Today we communicate through self-creation. Art today has indeed an indirect, but so much more important political function, because through art we can see, that things can always be done differently. There's always an alternative, while in politics there are often none. While in art you invent, in politics you decide. Political symbolism, no matter if leftist or rightist, is conservative. The national flag, the rose, the bird, or the pair of cherries as a communist party symbol all say: "Follow us, let yourself be led, because otherwise we don't need you at all!" Keeping these two worlds - art and politics in friction, that is what modern society stands and falls apart on. Not letting any political or any other form of social communication, from media commercials to seemingly exact economic prognosis lure you into total passivity. That is where I see the important function of creating art. Art in today's society is a specific form of structural irritation.

Art has its education system, its market, factories, agencies, stockholders, fairs, domains where profits and employees are being counted. Won't those who want to take on a fundamental and independent creative approach leave the art field at this time, when art has changed from a small, more or less autonomous domain into an industry?

Adorno used to attribute the culture industry with a sign of totality, absurd submission, prefabrication, and passivity. But he underestimated common human creativity. The fact that a person will never let anything be imposed upon himself without rests. Culture isn't only an industry, although it undoubtedly is crucially influenced by it. So today we can say that culture has primarily become entertainment. When we talk about the culture business, we have to mention the hazard, that art might become just a decoration, an ornament. Then it cannot resonate in public space. It is actually one of the many forms of today's all-penetrating depoliticisation:

"I am representing myself and I do not need to represent what is happening in society." But art will never be only private.

Don't you think that artists are reacting on current society way too much? Where is the abstraction that culminated Malevich's work? That wasn't so much about a relationship with society, it was about abstract and transcendental values. Abstraction was a part of modern thinking. Isn't today's artistic reaction to the world too specific? Just like the media and advertising?

I saw Emil Nolde's aquarelle exhibition last year in Bremen, which he created during fascism, when he wasn't allowed to exhibit publicly. He was travelling around Germany and one of the most admirable reflections of misery in Nazi society came only out of his personal need to create - a personal decision, which an artist was forced to make under violent political pressure, ultimately tells so much more about those times and society than any hard political production. But we can only tell in the course of time, comparing present to past. And also based on our current knowledge of that time in history.

But doesn't that also speak of incorrigibility? From this point of view we should already know that fifty years from now we won't see an exhibition of Saddam in formaldehyde because media images from these times will be more authentic.

Naturally there exists the danger that art will become overly contextual. I liked David Černý's *Saddam* in formaldehyde very much, but it is obvious that without the knowledge of a specific artistic and political context the purpose of such production quickly disappears. It lives in a moment just like twenty-four hour media coverage programs or commercials. But it needs to be said, that the same, maybe even bigger danger looms over conceptual and post conceptual art. Beuys' statement, that everyone is an artist, can be understood as a statement to provoke talents, to let out their creative energy, but naturally not everyone has the talent. So it's just one big lie. An illusion that could have led to the situation, which we began this interview with: that today there are just too many artists.

(translated into English by the Umělec magazine editor)

INDEX

INTRODUCTION

TOMÁŠ CÍSAŘOVSKÝ

STANISLAV DIVIŠ

JIŘÍ DAVID

PETR NIKL

Hatching I, 1986,
oil on canvas, 140 x 125 cm, p. 72
Little Horses, 1991,
oil on canvas, 162 x 145 cm, p. 75
Russula, 2001,
acrylic on canvas, 170 x 150 cm, p. 76
Anna as Pipi, 2004,
oil on canvas, 105 x 200 cm, p. 77
Filip Pointing, 2004,
oil on canvas, 190 x 150 cm, p. 80

PETR PÍSAŘÍK

Untitled, 2010,
mixed media on canvas,
110 x 80 cm, p. 84
Cuba libre, 2007,
mixed media – plastic, metal, wood,
110 x 45 x 73 cm, p. 87
Martian Revivalist, 2007–2008,
mixed media – plastic, metal, wood,
350 x 110 x 200 cm, p. 88
While I Was Tying a Bouquet,
mixed media on canvas on canvas,
160 x 75 cm, p. 91
Super Position, 2008,
mixed media on canvas,
250 x 250 cm, p. 92

JAN MERTA

Ideal Radiant III, 2000,
oil on canvas, 255 x 190 cm, p. 96
To the Welders /Farewell, Maestro/,
2000, oil on canvas, 220 x 190 cm, p. 99
Partner, (from the triptych Megi and Partner), 1999–2006,
acrylic on canvas, 160 x 135 cm, p. 100
Red Slum, 2002–2006,
oil on canvas, 195 x 361 cm, p. 102–103
Big Purchase, 1993,
acrylic on canvas, 200 x 240 cm, p. 105
Cottage /Red Bliss/, 2009,
acrylic on canvas, 300 x 195 cm, p. 107

JIŘÍ SURŮVKA

Gotham City, photo, 2009, p. 110
Twins, 1997,
airbrush on synthetic canvas,
100 x 100 cm, 2x, p. 112
Pineapple, 2008,
from the series Masters of War,
acrylic on canvas, 100 x 80 cm, p. 116
The Scream, 1996,
airbrush on synthetic canvas,
150 x 100 cm, p. 115

ANTONÍN STŘÍŽEK

Karlín, 2008,
oil on canvas, 130 x 110 cm, p. 122
Shoes, 1988,
acrylic on canvas, 162 x 218 cm, p. 125
Wild Geese, 1989,
oil on canvas, 100 x 70 cm, p. 126
Mácha, 1989,
45 x 55 cm, p. 129
Boys with Swans, 1998,
oil on canvas, 143 x 200 cm, p. 130

Also available through D.A.P. / Distributed Art Publishers
155 Sixth Avenue, 2nd Floor, New York, N.Y.10013, USA
Tel:++1(212)627-1999 Fax: ++1(212) 627-9484

PICTURES OF CZECH POSTMODERNISM

JIŘÍ PŘIBÁŇ

Ilustration and graphic design **Karel Štědrý**
Translation **Stuart Hoskins**
Photographs **Martin Polák**
Prepress KANT
Printing by Tiskárna Protisk s.r.o., České Budějovice
Publihed by KANT, 2013
kant@kant-books.com
www.kant-books.cz

ISBN: 978-80-7437-089-2

KANT

DONATH | CONSULTING

NO.MA

YOUR GUIDE
TO CONTEMPORARY
CZECH ART

www.no-ma.cz